75
Outrageous Ways

for Librarians to Impact Student Achievement in Grades K–8

Laurie Thelen

Library of Congress Cataloging-in-Publication Data

Thelen, Laurie Noble.
 75 outrageous ideas for librarians to impact student achievement : fun ideas to motivate students and inspire collaboration with national standards included / Laurie Thelen.
       p. cm.
 Includes bibliographical references and index.
 ISBN 1-58683-232-8 (pbk. : alk. paper) 1. Elementary school libraries--Activity programs--United States. 2. School librarian participation in curriculum planning--United States. 3. Education, Elementary--Activity programs--United States. 4. Motivation in education--United States. 5. Education--Standards--United States. I. Title. II. Title: Seventy-five outrageous ideas for librarians to impact student achievement.

 Z675.S3T458 2008
 027.62'6--dc22

                              2007026138

Published by Linworth Publishing, Inc.
3650 Olentangy River Rd, Suite 250
Columbus, OH 43214

1-58683-232-8

5 4 3 2 1

About the Author:

Laurie Thelen has enjoyed delivering an "outrageous" library program to the students at Deep Wood Elementary School in Round Rock, Texas, for the past six years. In elementary education for fifteen years, most of it in the library media center, she values the literature-literacy connection and the impact that library media specialists have on the lives of children. Besides reading she enjoys hiking and sketching in the Hill Country with her husband, Bob.

Dedication:

to Katheryn Noble, who always thought being a librarian looked like fun!

TABLE OF CONTENTS

TABLE OF FIGURES

INTRODUCTION

PURPOSE

Today, many librarians are calling upon their school community to acknowledge their leadership in education reform. No longer are we on the sidelines as part of the "support" services in the school building. We are librarians and teachers. As teachers we have an impact on student learning, not only in the language arts arena, but flooding over into all subject areas. No curricular area should be off limits to today's librarians. Collaborating, planning, and teaching by the library media specialist filters into science, math, social studies, health, and the fine arts. However, most of our school community does not see us in this light. They simply do not know what we can do. Library media specialists can impact and interact with student learning in provocative, new ways. The purpose of this book is to provide a resource of ideas that foster a unique, collaborative, and fun library media program that addresses student learning standards.

AUDIENCE

The audience for *75 Outrageous Ideas* is the elementary and middle school library media specialist. The person reading this book wants new ideas and is tired of the same old fundraisers, reading programs, collaboration units, and so on. New as well as experienced library media specialists can find useful ideas in this book.

ORGANIZATION

The book is organized into curricular areas with 75 ideas, big and small. Some ideas involve the whole school learning environment, while others can be used for specific grades and subject areas. Each is aligned with national standards in its curricular area. An assessment tool based on the national standards is included at the end of each activity. Remember, these ideas are to be done in concert with other members of the learning community: teachers, students, parents, and the at-large community.

NEED

Why is this book needed? The first need is impacting student learning. Demonstrating visibly how the library media center can help students learn within the district curriculum and guidelines is real job security. Our goal is to help students achieve their best. Another need is to deal with the time crunch we all face every day. This book was created as a quick, ready reference for the busy school library media specialist. Plus, deep down inside, we all want to have fun! The chapters provide jazzed-up collaboration units and large community-wide events.

The key is collaboration to fit these ideas into curriculum enhancement. That's why the first part of the book discusses ways to break into the collaborative mode with teachers and staff.

"Talk, talk, talk" is the mantra of the school library media specialist. Talk up the library program. Talk up new resources. Talk up ideas to help teachers. Classroom teachers often do not know how much the lounge, hallway, cafeteria, workroom, and the bathroom. No area is sacred to you. Shrug off the "no's" and keep on asking. Some of the best teachers to collaborate with are the new ones. They are desperate for any help.

The list below contains conversation to jump start the flow of ideas. Please notice none of these starters can be answered in "yes" or "no" responses.

1. **"Consider me your clone."**
   Every new teacher needs help, so seek these newbies out for great collaboration events.

2. **"I can help you teach that unit. When can we get together?"**
   Never ask *"Can we get together"* because teachers can easily say, "I'm too busy."

3. **"So, what great things are the kids learning in _____ (insert level grade)?"**
   This inquiry is very useful in the teacher's lounge and staff bathroom.

4. **"Let's have some fun and work on this together. I've got some great ideas for you."**
   If they know they will have a good time, they will come.

5. **"Hey, I can lighten the load for you on that unit."**
   Nothing speaks louder than time saved and a workload made easier.

6. **"Tell me about your plan for that unit."**
   The more you know, the more intelligent you can be with collaboration offers. Teachers want specifics on how you can make their lives easier.

TOOLS TO BEGIN COLLABORATION

The first tool is a useful planning form. Include the title of the unit, curriculum objectives and goals, corresponding content standards, date, and divisions of labor. Important to note is the inclusion of modifications for differentiated learning styles. The form can be paper or on the library Web page. See Figure I.1 for an example.

At the conclusion of the project, it is important to indicate student understanding on an assessment rubric. A spreadsheet to assist with data collection of student mastery of each of the units can be found at the end of each outrageous idea.

Start small and try a few of the ideas in the book the first year. Graduate to more and involve administrators, teachers, parents, students, and community members. Ask yourself at the end of the year: "Has the library media center's visibility increased after using one of these ideas?" The result is a powerful, outrageous library media center program.

Teacher and Librarian Collaboration Form

Teacher Name _____ date _____

Scheduled date for the unit/activity (single or range) _____

Total number of students _____

	STATE STANDARDS

Grade level (circle one)   K   1   2   3   4   5

Title of Unit Activity _____

Unit Goals and Objectives _____

_____

_____

_____

MODIFICATION OF ACTIVITIES

Learning Activities _____

_____

_____

_____

Classroom Teacher's Role   Library Media Specialist's Role

_____

_____

_____

_____

Comments _____

Figure I.1 Collaboration Form

CURRICULUM ACTIVITY LIST WITH GRADE LEVEL									
LANGUAGE ARTS	K	1	2	3	4	5	6	7	8
1. Hot Topics and Sizzling Research	✖	✖	✖	✖	✖	✖	✖	✖	✖
2. Multilingual Treasure Hunt				✖	✖	✖	✖	✖	✖
3. Poetry Slam Dunk					✖	✖	✖	✖	✖
4. Recipe-a-Rama			✖	✖	✖	✖	✖		
5. Stations of Book Talks					✖	✖	✖	✖	✖
6. A Summary Is Like a Hamburger				✖	✖	✖	✖	✖	✖
7. Walking Word Walls	✖	✖	✖						
8. Writing Workshop	✖	✖	✖	✖	✖	✖	✖	✖	✖
9. Monster Read-In	✖	✖	✖	✖	✖	✖	✖		
10. Theme-a-Rama	✖	✖	✖	✖	✖	✖	✖	✖	✖
SCIENCE	K	1	2	3	4	5	6	7	8
11. Adopt a Worm			✖	✖	✖	✖	✖		
12. Create Your Own Planet	✖	✖	✖	✖	✖	✖	✖	✖	✖
13. Rocks, Soil, and Water	✖	✖							
14. Let Go My Eco				✖	✖	✖	✖	✖	✖
15. Pirate Treasure in the Library					✖	✖	✖		
16. Science Camp						✖	✖	✖	✖
17. Science-Telling	✖	✖	✖	✖	✖	✖	✖	✖	✖
18. Will It Float?	✖	✖	✖	✖	✖				
19. Science Rocks Reading Incentive Program				✖	✖	✖	✖	✖	✖
20. Science Career Day						✖	✖	✖	✖
21. A Night under the Stars	✖	✖	✖	✖	✖	✖	✖	✖	✖
MATH	K	1	2	3	4	5	6	7	8
22. Dewey Demystification				✖	✖	✖	✖	✖	✖
23. Graph It!				✖	✖	✖	✖	✖	✖
24. The Kids Who Measured the School					✖	✖	✖	✖	✖
25. Math Around the World			✖	✖	✖	✖	✖	✖	✖
26. Math Garden	✖	✖	✖	✖	✖	✖	✖	✖	✖
27. Math Magic Bags	✖	✖	✖	✖	✖	✖	✖	✖	✖
28. Percentage Quest				✖	✖	✖	✖	✖	✖
29. Poster Math	✖	✖	✖	✖	✖	✖	✖	✖	✖
30. Number Collage PK	✖	✖							

Fig. I.2 Curriculum Activity List with Grade Level

75 Outrageous Ways for Librarians to Impact Student Achievement in Grades K – 8

MATH	K	1	2	3	4	5	6	7	8
31. Fruit Loop® Math PK	✖	✖							
32. Egg Math	✖	✖	✖	✖	✖	✖	✖	✖	✖
33. Calculator Activity	✖	✖	✖	✖	✖	✖	✖	✖	✖
34. Biggest and Smallest			✖	✖					
35. The Big Tree			✖	✖	✖	✖			
36. Book Measuring		✖	✖	✖	✖	✖			
37. Tangram Activity			✖	✖	✖	✖			
38. Story Problem Challenge			✖	✖	✖	✖			
39. Shop Until You Drop				✖	✖	✖	✖	✖	✖
MUSIC, VISUAL ARTS, AND THEATRE	K	1	2	3	4	5	6	7	8
40. Artful Learning Ideas	✖	✖	✖	✖	✖	✖	✖	✖	✖
41. Get Graphic!						✖	✖	✖	✖
42. Music Connection	✖	✖	✖	✖	✖	✖	✖	✖	✖
43. Picture Book Artists	✖	✖	✖	✖	✖	✖	✖	✖	✖
44. Readers Theater Scripts	✖	✖	✖	✖	✖	✖	✖	✖	✖
45. Artists Helping Children	✖	✖	✖	✖	✖	✖	✖	✖	✖
SOCIAL STUDIES	K	1	2	3	4	5	6	7	8
46. Connect with the World					✖	✖	✖	✖	✖
47. Guinness Gotcha Game					✖	✖	✖	✖	✖
48. Kamishibai Stories	✖	✖	✖	✖	✖	✖	✖	✖	✖
49. Living Wax Museum					✖	✖	✖	✖	✖
50. Odd Inventions	✖	✖	✖	✖	✖	✖	✖	✖	✖
51. World Cultures Night	✖	✖	✖	✖	✖	✖	✖	✖	✖
52. Adopt a School in Africa	✖	✖	✖	✖	✖	✖	✖	✖	✖
53. The Mercy Corps and The Hunger Site	✖	✖	✖	✖	✖	✖	✖	✖	✖
54. Save the Children	✖	✖	✖	✖	✖	✖	✖	✖	✖
TECHNOLOGY	K	1	2	3	4	5	6	7	8
55. Broadcast News					✖	✖	✖	✖	✖
56. Create an ezine						✖	✖	✖	✖
57. Connected Tech	✖	✖	✖	✖	✖	✖	✖	✖	✖
58. Smart Board® Ideas				✖	✖	✖	✖	✖	✖
59. Microsoft Photo Story 3® Software					✖	✖	✖	✖	✖

Fig. I.2 Curriculum Activity List with Grade Level

Chapter 1

OUTRAGEOUS LANGUAGE ARTS IDEAS

INTRODUCTION

Our goal as library media specialists is to create thinkers as well as readers. Promoting critical-thinking skills is crucial to the process of developing students' learning. We must inspire them to interact with the text they see before them, in any media format. This interaction with words can be made user friendly by developing methods to explore and organize text efficiently. One of the best ways to accomplish this is through research projects that stress the gradual development of questioning skills. The example in this chapter involves students in the creation of their own research question and results in the astonishing concept of student ownership of the research process.

COLLABORATION EVENTS

1. Hot Topics and Sizzling Research

Grades: K – 8

STANDARDS				
Information Literacy	1	2	3	4
English Language Arts	8	12		

Fig. 1.1 Hot Topics and Sizzling Research Standards

In this project, the students decide what they want to research. The teacher chooses the broad area, such as animal behavior. Students are free to form "I wonder…" questions within this broad area. This type of research will transform the information- seeking process. Students become excited because they have ownership of their sizzling question. The library media specialist's collaborative role with the teacher includes the following:

- information process design
- preliminary teaching of questioning strategies
- decoding nonfiction text
- information sources and search strategies
- evaluation of the completed projects

Session 1: Model, Model, Model

The library media specialist brings in artifacts and articles based on an interest to model independent research inquiry. Tell how an interesting subject leads to learning more and to research. A musical instrument is a useful tool to demonstrate the research process. Research questions using a mandolin include:

What is the history of the mandolin?

Who first played the mandolin?

Is the mandolin used for classical or folk music?

What gives the mandolin its unique sound?

Is the mandolin played in popular music today?

Discuss "I Wonder ..." Questions

"I wonder ..." questions begin the process of questioning. Give examples from your own interests. Ask students for their own examples in the discussion. Often students become confused at this juncture. Formulating high-level questions is a difficult task. To stimulate the process, create the question cubes below.

Supplies

Use die-cut box patterns or create a larger box with the following supplies:

Foam Board

X-acto™ Cutting Knife

Tape

Markers

Directions

Two cube sets will be made for each student. The following directions are for one cube. Cut six square shapes all the same size, for example four inches by four inches. Tape four squares together. Add the additional squares to the top and bottom to create a cube.

Write the following words on one set of the cube faces:

Compare	Why
Contrast	Cause
Differentiate	Effect

Write the following words on the other cube faces:

Invent	Discover
Explain	Critique
What if ...	Recommend

Modeling with an area of interest, roll one die. For example, if a student is interested in cars, a good question might be "How can I compare the gas mileage and the lowest price to find the best car to buy?"

Session 2: "Fat" and "Skinny" Question Discussion

Some questions can be answered too easily and others lead to more in depth research. "Skinny" questions are who, what, where, when, and how questions. "Fat" questions are higher-level thinking questions that begin with compare, contrast, analyze, evaluate. See Figure 1.2 and 1.3 for PowerPoint® slide examples of differentiating between lower- and higher-level questions. As the questions are read, students decide if each one belongs in the "fat" box or the "skinny" box. After this exercise, students break into small groups to analyze the questions they formed about their research topic. The classroom teacher and the library media specialist visit each table to monitor student discussion and critique questions.

More examples of higher-level thinking skills can be found at St. Edward's University's task-oriented question construction wheel based on Bloom's Taxonomy. <www.stedwards.edu/cte/resources/bwheel.htm>

Decoding Nonfiction Text

QUESTIONS

What do lemurs eat?

How long do boa constrictors get?

What part of the world do rattlesnakes live in?

How are kangaroos and wallabies alike and different?

How do scientists know that mammoths and elephants are related?

How are butterflies and moths alike and different?

How many different types of snakes are there in the world?

Why do dogs bark?

How can I train my dog, Rascal, to stop growling at my bigger dog, Buddy?

How do vets tell how old dogs are if they don't know the dogs' birthday?

I have a dog named Bowman. His eyes run all the time. Should I take him to the vet? Is it a serious problem?

Why do my dogs dig up my backyard? Can I stop them from doing it?

How long have potters been making raku pottery? What techniques did they use to fire the pots?

What can I do to get rid of my dog's bad breath?

What are some of the theories about why the dinosaurs are extinct?

What evidence do scientists have to back up their theories?

Figure 1.2 Questions to Consider

SKINNY **QUESTIONS**   FAT **QUESTIONS**

Figure 1.3 Question Categories

Reading nonfiction takes special skills. The pre-decoding skills involve looking for any large type and pictures on the page. The next step is to read captions under pictures, graphs, or tables, and sub-headings within the material. Finally, reading each section under the sub-headings and taking notes, both mental and written, is critical. The goal of the library media specialist at this step is to form a link between the written word and the student. Asking, "What does this say to me?" or "Does this answer my research question?" after each paragraph helps students to determine a link from the text to their research question. See Figure 1.4 for useful tips on reading nonfiction.

HINTS FOR READING NONFICTION TEXT

MAGAZINES AND ENCYCLOPEDIAS

– Ask

Are there any pictures on the page?

What do the title and the subtitles say?

Can I find the answers to my questions after reading the subtitles?

DATABASES AND INTERNET INFORMATION:

– Ask *(see questions above)*

– Use the FIND shortcut: <hold down the CTRL key and the F key>

Figure 1.4 Tips to Decode Nonfiction

Session 3: Note-Taking

A helpful graphic organizer for students to use for note-taking can be found in Figure 1.5.

Name: Date:	Research Question 1	Research Question 2	Research Question 3
Source 1 A. B. C. D. E.			

Figure 1.5 Graphic Organizer for Notes

On the page, each resource has an alphabet letter that stands for information to be used in a bibliography.

A: Author (Last name, first name)

B: Book Title (or article/Web page title)

C: City and Company (Example: New York: American Publishing Books, Inc.)

D: Date (Example: 2006)

E: Every page I used. (Example: pp. 24-34)

The note-taking form allows for further questions to be developed after the material is read.

Project Product

The classroom teacher and library media specialist develop a rubric to help students choose a product to demonstrate the answers to their research questions, such as a newspaper article, story, brochure, or a PowerPoint® presentation.

Assessment Rubric

SKILL	LEVEL I Minimum	LEVEL II Average	LEVEL III Excellent
Did the students form higher-level questions?			
Were the students able to evaluate resources and take notes efficiently?			
Did the students complete the products?			

Figure 1.6 Research Assessment Rubric

2. Multilingual Treasure Hunt

Grades: 3–8

Working with language dictionaries, classmates, teachers, and parents, decipher mysterious library messages.

FOREIGN LANGUAGE EDUCATION STANDARDS	
1.2	4.1

Fig. 1.7 Foreign Language Education Standards

Create messages in different languages on a bulletin board and challenge students, in pairs, to translate the words. Use online and paper language dictionaries. Incentives include a free bookmark, pencil, or eraser.

Free translation Web sites include:

<http://babelfish.altavista.com>
<http://www.google.com/language_tools?hl=en>

Assessment Rubric

SKILL	LEVEL I Minimum	LEVEL II Average	LEVEL III Excellent
Is the translation clear?			
Is there a connection between text and message?			

Figure 1.8 Multilingual Treasure Hunt Assessment Rubric

3. Poetry Slam Dunk

Grades: 4–8

NATIONAL COUNCIL OF TEACHERS OF ENGLISH			
Standards for the English Language Arts	2	4	5

Figure 1.9 National Standards for the Poetry Slam Dunk

The Poetry Slam Dunk project involves five sessions. Each session builds upon poetry skills and culminates in a poetry performance. Each session can be done on sequential days or once a week.

Materials

Books
Sports Equipment and Memorabilia

Session 1

The classroom teacher and library media specialist introduce the Poetry Slam Dunk. Read *Karate Kid* by Jane Yolen in *Opening Days: Sports Poems* compiled by editor Lee Bennet Hopkins. To jump start inspiration, ask the following questions:

• Name objects that poet Jane Yolen compares with karate positions.

• How does the author convey movement in the poem?

• Notice the rhyming words. Where does the poet use these words?

The classroom teacher or library media specialist creates an "I am …" poem with the class. Ask students for a sports suggestion. Create a word bank of descriptive words for the chosen sport. Spark discussion with these questions: "What is the body doing in the sport?" "Can we compare the movement in the sport with something different, such as in Jane Yolen's *Karate Kid*?"

Session 2

Read poetry selections in *Read a Rhyme, Write a Rhyme* by Jack Prelutsky. A few of the poems provide starting stanzas, as well as a word bank to finish the poem. Ask for suggestions of favorite sports.

Session 3

Students will complete the Poetry Web Quest (see page 15) in the classroom or library media center. Working in pairs, students explore and create poetry.

Session 4

Visit classrooms with a placard that reads "Poetry Slam Dunk Time." Read more poems from the following suggested book list:

Slam Dunk: Basketball Poems by Lillian Morrison

That Sweet Diamond: Baseball Poems by Paul B. Janeczko

Extra Innings: Baseball Poems by Lee Bennett Hopkins (editor)

Fantastic Football Poems by John Foster

Ere We Go! An Anthology of Football Poems by David Orme

Girls Got Game! Sports Stories and Poems by Sue Macy

Provide time during the classroom language arts period for a critique of the student's presentation, such as volume of voice, facial expression, gestures, and stance.

Session 5

On the day of the contest, set aside an area for a simple stage. Decorate with sports memorabilia, such as pennants, basketball nets, and balls. Students may designate a pinch hitter (a substitute reader) if they are too shy to read their poem aloud. Students who write a poem are rewarded with free tickets to a sports game or free promotional gear. If there is no local team, contact the local high school to reserve a special section for the poets.

Assessment Rubric

SKILL	LEVEL I: Minimum	LEVEL II: Average	LEVEL III: Excellent
Week 1 Does the student participate in discussion and critique of poetry samples?			
Week 2 Does the student contribute to the writing process in the completion of stanzas?			
Week 3 Does the student use poetic devices to construct a poem?			
Week 4 Does the student participate in the Poetry Slam?			

Figure 1.10 Poetry Slam Dunk Assessment Rubric

Poetry Web Quest

You will be going to the following sites to complete the activities as listed below. If you want, you can copy this page so you have the directions in front of you.

What is Poetry?

Types of Poetry . . . . <www.shadowpoetry.com/resources/wip/types.html>

Click on the Web site above to learn about all the different types. Click on several buttons to learn more about each one.

Learn to Rhyme

Rhyming Dictionary . . . .

Pick a word that you might use to describe yourself. Submit the word to find rhyming possibilities. Write an eight-line poem with two stanzas using one of your rhyming words in each line. Open a word processing document to write your poem. Copy the poem into your folder.

Create Your Own Poem

Poetry Place: . . . . <http://www.poem.freeservers.com/design.htm>

Play around with the words to create your own unique poem. Print out the finished product.

Learn about Poets . . . . <www.poets.org/poet.php/prmPID/68>

Search the database for a poet that you like.

- Open a word processing document and write a short informational bio about him or her. Also include why you like the poetry.
- Copy and paste a picture of him or her.
- Copy and paste the words to a poem by this person. Print this out to share with the class.

RESOURCES

Poetry Aloud Here! Sharing Poetry with Children in the Library by Sylvia M. Vardell
Wishes, Lies, and Dreams: Teaching Children to Write Poetry by Kenneth Koch, Ron Padgett
Favorite Poetry Lessons by Paul Janeczko

4. Recipe-a-Rama

Grades: 2–6

Study the recipe writing technique with students. No other form of writing demands as much clarity and exactness in the writing process.

NATIONAL STANDARDS			
Informational Literacy	3		
English Language Arts	2	5	9

Figure 1.11 National Standards for Recipe-a-Rama

After reading a cookbook or investigating recipes on the Internet, solicit student response about the format, style, and language of a recipe. Remember, accuracy is the key component to recipe construction. Point out the list of ingredients and the directions for construction of the recipe. Discuss what would happen if an ingredient were missing. Ask students to work in pairs with chart paper to recall a favorite recipe and write down the ingredients. Results will be interesting as students try to remember the ingredients and the formula for the construction of the dish. For additional extension of the activity, students interview their parents or guardians about how to make their favorite food and bring recipes together for a class cookbook.

Internet Resources

              <www.easy-kids-recipes.com>
              <pbskids.org/zoom/activities/cafe>
              <www.sandiegozoo.org/kids/recipes.html>
              <www.sallys-place.com/food/ethnic_cusine/ethnic_cusine.htm>

Assessment Rubric

SKILL	LEVEL I: Minimum	LEVEL II: Average	LEVEL III: Excellent
Is the recipe accurate?			
Does the recipe follow the writing format?			

Figure 1.12 Recipe-a-Rama Assessment Rubric

5. Stations of Book Talks

Grades: 3–8

    Place students around the library to give quick book talks. Book talking involves summarization activities for students. The mechanics of a book talk are as follows:

- Keep the book talk brief—only two to three minutes.
- Grab the readers with an interesting part at the front of the book.
- Connect your listeners to the book with problems they may be facing.
- Read a climactic part of the book, but do not reveal the end.
- Use props to keep interest alive.

An excellent Web resource for student book talks can be found at
        <www.bcps.org/offices/lis/models/bktalk>

6. A Summary Is Like a Hamburger

Grades: 3–8

NATIONAL COUNCIL OF TEACHERS OF ENGLISH	
Standards for the English Language Arts	3

Figure 1.13 National Standards for A Summary is Like a Hamburger

One of the most difficult concepts in the language arts arena is summarization. It's a high-level skill and takes constant reinforcement by everyone, including the library media specialist. Asking for a summary after a read-aloud book is a great start, but the "outrageous" librarian goes a step further with a PowerPoint® presentation with a mnemonic device, "A Summary Is Like a Hamburger" (Figure 1.14).

Slide 1: Summarization	**Slide 2:** **What is a Summary?** Briefly restates the **main idea.** Includes only **the most important details** Shows how the important details are **connected.** *A good summary tells what the whole story is about!* **Main idea + Important details = Summary**
Slide 3: End Meaty Part: Important Details Beginning	**Slide 4:** **Why do I need to Summarize?** To help you understand what you read. To improve your research skills. Plus, it helps you remember information for a test!
Slide 5: **Summary Session:** Read aloud *Pete's a Pizza!* by William Steig	**Slide 6:** **What are the important details in each section?** Who? What? Where? When? How? Why?

Figure 1.14 "A Summary is Like a Hamburger" PowerPoint

Slide 7:	Slide 8:
Choose the best summary for *Pete's a Pizza*.	**The correct answer is:**
A. Pete giggles when his parents "knead the dough." Pete tells them they are not supposed to tickle their "pizza." His father tells him that pizzas are not supposed to laugh. B. To cure Pete's bad mood because of the rain, his father decides to make a "pizza" of him. He has so much fun when his parents add pepperoni, cheese, knead, and "bake" him, that he soon forgets about the rainy day. C. To make Pete into a pizza, his father adds talcum powder for flour, water for oil, checkers for tomatoes, and paper for cheese. Then his parents "bake" him in the oven, which is the couch. D. Always play a game with your child when they are in a bad mood. Pete had a lot of fun and then the rain stopped.	**B**

Figure 1.14 "A Summary is Like a Hamburger" PowerPoint

Assessment Rubric

SKILL	LEVEL I Minimum	LEVEL II Average	LEVEL III Excellent
Can the student describe the parts of a summary?			
Can the student effectively determine summary statements for brief articles?			

Figure 1.15 A Summary Is like a Hamburger Assessment Rubric

7. Walking Word Walls

Grades: K–2

NATIONAL STANDARDS FOR THE ENGLISH LANGUAGE ARTS	
3	4

Figure 1.16 National Standards for Walking Word Walls

Before reading a story, write the new vocabulary words on large index cards. Read the word in the context of the story and ask students to think of a kid-friendly definition. Read the story and pause at each new word and discuss its meaning. If the new word expresses an emotion, ask students to show it facially. After reading the story, ask students to draw a picture of one of the new words. Write the word on one side of a poster board. Glue the picture to another piece of poster board and wear as a sandwich board. Walk

75 Outrageous Ways for Librarians to Impact Student Achievement in Grades K – 8

through the halls with the sandwich board and ask, "Have you heard? There's a new word." Point to the word and ask for a definition. Also, place the picture and definition on a PowerPoint® slide show for the daily student broadcast.

Assessment Rubric

SKILL	LEVEL I Minimum	LEVEL II Average	LEVEL III Excellent
Did the student use strategies to comprehend word meaning?			
Did the student use the new vocabulary correctly in the drawing?			

Figure 1.17 Walking Word Walls Assessment Rubric

8. Writing Workshop

Grades: K–8

Time: One day to a week, depending on age group

NATIONAL STANDARDS FOR THE ENGLISH LANGUAGE ARTS			
2	4	5	6

Figure 1.18 National Standards for Writing Workshop

Make the library media center a partner with classroom writing experiences. Collaborate with teachers on grade levels to make the library a stop on the writing stations in the classroom.

- The classroom teacher reads a book to students and discusses story construction, such as setting, plot, characters, problem, sequence of events, and final solution. The teacher defines the writing project and clearly states what will be assessed: author voice, character development, a discernible plot, sequence of events, continuity, and resolution of events in the story.

- The library media specialist reads the first few pages of a book with a great beginning, such as The Library by Sarah Stewart or The True Story of the Three Little Pigs by Jon Scieszka. The class as a whole comes up with an alternate ending. Model the following with students: sentence construction, capitalization, and punctuation.

- Working in groups determined by the teacher, provide students with the beginnings of stories familiar to them, such as fairy tales. Together students construct alternate endings. The teacher and library media specialist teach how to function in a writing group by modeling a writing session for the students.

- In the classroom, this activity is extended. When students are finished writing their endings, they meet in peer editing groups of four children and read their story. An extension activity for upper grades is a daily writing prompt for a week-long camp.

- For the camp, students bring in beach towels or sleeping bags and sit on the floor to work and critique first draft writing samples. Camp T-shirts can be easy and low cost. Create a design on a word processor and then print it out. The students turn the design to the wrong side and color with fabric crayons. Each student takes their completed drawing home and an adult irons the design on to a white T-shirt, colored side down.

- The teacher and library media specialist conduct conference and evaluation sessions throughout the writing process. Peer review is equally important throughout all phases of the writing experience. Students gather together periodically to listen to one another's narratives and provide feedback to the writer.

When the writing is revised the students are ready to "hire" illustrators, other members of the classroom. After illustrations are complete, the book is bound by staples or with a spiral binding and presented to the student.

The library media center then hosts an Author's Party to celebrate the writers. Create a special Author's Chair for students to sit in to read their stories. Inexpensive chairs can be bought at garage sales or thrift stores and decorated with paint, fabric, jeweled sequins, and many other items. The Author's Chair can be used during the peer editing group time if the student needs advice, too.

Assessment Rubric

SKILL	LEVEL I Minimum	LEVEL II Average	LEVEL III Excellent
Does the student participate in the peer writing group?			
Does the student contribute to the critiquing process in the peer editing group?			
Does the student use a variety of strategies in the writing process?			
Does the student demonstrate a knowledge of language structure and convention?			

Figure 1. 19 Writing Workshop Assessment Rubric

Resources

Never Too Early to Write: Adventures in the K-1 Writing Workshop by Madeline Johnson
25 Mini-Lessons for Teaching Writing by Adele Fiderer (Grades 3–6)
Just Write!: Ten Practical Workshops for Successful Student Writing by Sylvia Gunnrey(Grades 7–12)
6 + 1 Traits of Writing: The Complete Guide (Grades 3 and Up) by Ruth Culham
50 Writing Lessons That Work!: Motivating Prompts and Easy Activities That Develop the Essentials of Strong Writing (Grades 4–8) by Carol Rawlings Miller
Because Writing Matters: Improving Student Writing in Our Schools by The National Writing Project, Carl Nagin – professional advice

READING INCENTIVE PROGRAMS

The next section of the language arts chapter lists reading programs. One of the keys to developing students who appreciate literature is to sponsor school-wide reading programs. Beginning the school year with a reading emphasis is an excellent way to jump-start student reading.

9. Monster Read-In (large community reading program)   Grades: K–6

NATIONAL STANDARDS			
INFORMATION LITERACY	5		
ENGLISH LANGUAGE ARTS	3	5	12

Figure 1.20 National Standards for Monster Read-In

Conduct storytimes with a monster theme. Read *Leonardo the Terrible Monster* by Mo Willems. Ask the student, "What makes a monster? What would a Reading Monster do?"

Invite students to participate in a Monster Read-In. Books do not have to be on the subject of monsters, however. Each student reads for a set time in minutes to qualify for the reward. Younger students can read with or be read to by a parent, grandparent, siblings, or guardian. Older students can count the time they read to their younger siblings, too. Conduct a writer's workshop after the reading program is completed to create class monster books. Emphasize plot, characters, setting, problem, and solution. Use chart paper and staple them together for each class.

Print Resources (alphabetical order)

Kindergarten through Second Grade (alphabetical order):
The Adventures of the Bailey School Kids series by Debbie Dadey
Everything I Know about Monsters: A Collection of Made-Up Facts, Educated Guesses, and Silly Pictures about Creatures of Creepiness by Tom Lichtenheld
Glad Monsters, Sad Monsters by Anne Miranda
Go Away, Big Green Monster by Ed Emberley
How to Draw 101 Monsters (How to Draw) by Dan Green
Junie B. Jones Has a Monster under Her Bed by Barbara Park
Little Monster series by Mercer Mayer
Monster Goose by Judy Sierra
Monster Museum by Marilyn Singer
The Monster Who Ate My Peas by Danny Schnitzlein
My Monster Mama Loves Me So by Laura Leuck
One Monster after Another by Mercer Mayer

Third Grade through Eighth Grade (alphabetical order):
The Boggart and the Monster by Susan Cooper
Deltora Book of Monsters by Emily Rodda
Goosebumps series by R. L. Stine

Here Be Monsters by Alan Snow
How to Draw 101 Monsters (How to Draw) by Dan Green
The Monsters of Morley Manor: A Madcap Adventure by Bruce Coville
Monsters: The World's Most Incredible Animals by Beatrice Fontanel
Mythological Monsters of Ancient Greece by Sara Fanelli
Tales from the Odyssey: Sirens and Sea Monsters by Mary Pope Osborne

The minute requirements for each grade level are listed below:

K: 50, 1st: 100, 2nd: , 3rd: 200, 4th: 300, 5th: 400, 6th: 500

MONSTER READ-IN PROGRAM!

Devour as many books as you can!

Name: _____

Grade: _____   Teacher: _____

TITLES	Parent/Guardian or Teacher Initials
_____	_____
_____	_____
_____	_____
_____	_____
_____	_____
_____	_____
_____	_____
_____	_____

Figure 1.21 Monster Read-In Form

Reward!

Place plastic game pieces in a bucket filled with toy slime with the following words written on them:

Library Reading Free Time

Extra Books

Bookmark

When students have completed the reading log, they place their hand into the slime bucket to retrieve a prize!

Assessment Rubric

SKILL	LEVEL I: Minimum	LEVEL II: Average	LEVEL III: Excellent
QUALITATIVE DATA: SURVEY RESULTS			
QUANTITATIVE DATA: PARTICIPATION LEVEL			

Figure 1.22 Monster Read-In Program Assessment Rubric

Survey

For younger students, use the survey in Figure 1.23 and a verbal interview.

QUALITATIVE DATA:

1. Did you enjoy the titles you read?

☐ Yes   ☐ No   ☐ Some

2. Could you write a monster story of your own after reading the titles?

☐ Yes   ☐ No

3. Would you recommend any titles to others?

☐ Yes   ☐ No

List some of the books you enjoyed:_____

_____

_____

Figure 1.23 Monster Read-in Program Survey

10. Theme-a-Rama

Grades: K–8

Pick a theme for an entire semester or year.

NATIONAL STANDARDS		
INFORMATIONAL LITERACY	5	
ENGLISH LANGUAGE ARTS	1	2

Figure 1.24 National Standards for Theme-a-Rama Reading Program

One theme idea is "Monkey Around in the Library." At the first school assembly program of the new school year, go on stage looking for readers who want to hang out in the library. Don a pair of binoculars, grab a safari hat, and wear khaki for the full affect. Monthly events are based on the theme, such as:

- Bring in zookeepers with exotic animals
- Contact artists that create with woven or natural fibers
- Instruct students on how to build a tiki hut
- Bring in local science professionals to tell about the rainforest ecology
- Hold a local Community Clean-Up Fundraiser (see Offbeat Fundraising, Chapter 10)

Readers participate in a timed reading program, such as 100 minutes. Reward students at various time intervals:

K – 100 minutes	3 – 400 minutes
1 – 200 minutes	4 – 500 minutes
2 – 300 minutes	5 – 600 minutes.

This reading program should last at least three months. When the students have finished reading they receive a trip to the Treasure Box filled with rainforest themed prizes.

Other theme ideas can be based on state award booklists. Simply choose a book on the list, decorate the library media center, and host a reading program. "Discover Reading" is a theme based on a state reading list that included Lewis and Clark's expedition of North America.

For more themes, look at the resources available at <www.highsmith.com>.

 Assessment Rubric

SKILL	Level I Minimum	LEVEL II Average	LEVEL III Excellent
Did the students complete the minutes read in the time period?			
Are students able to discuss the book?			

Figure 1.25 Theme-a-Rama Assessment Rubric

Chapter 2

OUTRAGEOUS SCIENCE IDEAS

INTRODUCTION

How is science connected to the library media center? Certainly there are science books and materials on the library shelves, but the "outrageous" librarian goes beyond just books. Involvement in the curriculum and ultimately in student objectives in the testing arena lend the impetus to bring science off the shelves and into real experiences. Obviously, the library media center cannot be turned into a science laboratory, but library media specialists can demonstrate quite a few science truths with some creative twists.

COLLABORATION

11. Adopt a Worm

Grades: 2–6

NATIONAL SCIENCE EDUCATION		
LIFE SCIENCE STANDARDS	K-4	5-8
NATIONAL EDUCATIONAL TECHNOLOGY		
4 a. TECHNOLOGY COMMUNICATION TOOLS		

Figure 2.1 National Standards for Adopt a Worm

Step 1: Reading Text

Read *Diary of a Worm* by Doreen Cronin. Discuss the characteristics of fiction and nonfiction works:

- Is *Diary of a Worm* fiction or nonfiction? What about the book tells you it is fiction?

- Is there a hint from the drawings that this book might be fiction?

- What about the content: do earthworms go to school or talk?

Hold up a nonfiction companion book such as:

- *Wiggling Worms at Work* by John Himmelman

- *Earthworm* by Lee Jacobs

- *I Wonder What It's Like Being an Earthworm* by Erin M. Hovanec

Ask the students to determine if the book is fiction or nonfiction based on a first, quick look at the book. *Wiggling Worms at Work* and *An Earthworm's Life* can be difficult to determine if one looks only at the illustrations. Sometimes nonfiction books use photographs, but it is not a reliable indicator of the content of the book. Do the illustrations reveal facts or a story? Read a page and ask the students if the content sounds like fiction or nonfiction. Complete the reading of a nonfiction book on earthworms to prepare the class for an observation of real earthworms.

Step 2: What Do Earthworms Do All Day? Grades: 1–3

Supplies and Equipment

- **WormVue Wonder Kit** ($27.95) by HSP Nature Toys

Complete kit includes: Double-sided viewing unit with shield and tray (keeps light out – worms in), live action experiment booklet, facts and anatomy poster, worm cutouts, magnifying glass, growing tray, litmus paper and cups. Mail-in certificate, plus $7.95, for 200 live worms, three types of soil layers, worm castings, and food. Available from <http://www.stevespanglerscience.com>

- Pencil

Directions

Set up the WormVue kit according to manufacturer's directions. After reading *Wiggling Worms at Work* and *Diary of a Worm*, show students the worm kit. Tell students they will be creating an online journal, or blog, of what the earthworms do each day.

The library media specialist assists the classroom teacher with instruction in Internet use protocol, research of the elements of an online journal or blog, and evaluation of the material to be included in the blog. Setting up a blog for the first time has been made easy by <www.blogger.com>. At this site, a blog can be created in 10 simple steps. The novice blogger can choose <Blogspot.com> as the location of the blog; however, it is advertising-supported. The more experienced can give <Blogger.com> the FTP address of the Web site for the location of the blog.

Supplies and Equipment

- SMART Board®
- Projector
- Screen
- Laptop
- Web page creation software, such as FrontPage® by Microsoft™, installed on computers

Directions

1. Define blog for the students: a blog, or Web log, is a shared online journal where people can post diary entries about their personal experiences and hobbies.
2. Show an example of a classroom blog or diary: <http://twinlakes.k12.in.us/schools/elem/el/mrgall/diary/diary.html>.
3. Discuss the components of a journal or diary. If students have kept diaries or journals, ask them to tell about the experience. Students will be summarizing activities, so define summary for them. A summary is a short sentence or paragraph that tells all about an event.
4. Model journal writing on the SMART Board® using the daily blog worksheet, shown in Figure 3.5, to help gather the daily activities. Type the date, followed by a colon, and write a sentence. Students may use first names as in the Web diary example, but last names should never be used for security reasons.

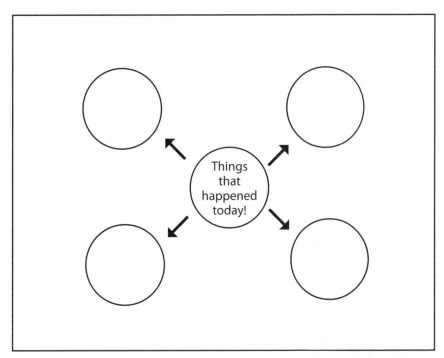

Figure 2.2 Worm Blog Form

5. If there is no time for a daily blog, choose one day of the week for students to summarize the week's activities.

6. Divide the class into groups of four to five students. Each group will be responsible for writing that day 's or week's summary of activities. Students will do a rough draft in Microsoft Word®. Meet with the group to assess their writing.

 ## Assessment Rubric

This rubric will be used when the teacher or library media specialist meets with the writing group of the day or week.

Student Name:					
Facts included?					
Internet manners used?					
Grammar and Spelling?					

Figure 2.3 Worm Blog Assessment Rubric

12. Create Your Own Planet

All grade levels

NATIONAL SCIENCE EDUCATION STANDARDS	
CONTENT STANDARD D: Earth and Space	K-4

Figure 2.4 National Standards for Create Your Own Planet

One of the best Web sites to introduce the solar system is Planet 10 created by Planet Science <http://www.solarsystem.org.uk/planet10>. Planet 10 is an interactive Web site which includes a Solar System fly-through and helps to build a new planet in the Solar System (see Figure 2.5).

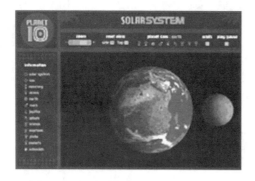

Figure 2.5 Planet 10 Web Site

When students click on World Builder they will be given a chance to create a new planet: physical characteristics, surface and atmosphere, population, orbit, and pathway. Students name the planet and launch it into the solar system to see if it will survive.

 Assessment Rubric

SKILL	LEVEL I Minimum	LEVEL II Average	LEVEL III Excellent
Did the new planet survive?			
What characteristics were found to be most favorable for planet survival?			

Figure 2.6 Planet 10 Assessment Rubric

13. Rocks, Soil, and Water: An earth science collaboration unit with kindergarten students

Grade: K–1 (2 or 3 sessions)

NATIONAL SCIENCE EDUCATION STANDARDS	
EARTH AND SPACE	K-4

Figure 2.7 National Standards for Rocks, Soil, and Water

Session 1

Meet with the kindergarten teachers and decide the research questions to be studied. Choose a final product to evaluate understanding. Pre-select materials (videos, books, etc.).

Session 2

Present the PowerPoint® "Rocks, Soil, and Water" (Figure 2.8), reading aloud each section. Using a SMART Board®, write down the answer to the "KWL" responses. Stop after the "Information Quest" slide. Model reading for information seeking. Instruct students to hold a "thumbs up" if they hear an answer to the research question. Pause after reading each sentence and ask students for a response. If one is heard, go back to the slide "Research Questions" and write down the information.

Slide 1: **Rocks, Soil, and Water**	Slide 2: **KWL Research** - **K:** Write down everything you already **know** about your research question. - **W:** List **what** you need to find to answer your research question. - **L:** What did you **learn** after you researched your question?
Slide 3: **K:** **Let's write down everything you know about rocks, soil, and water:**	Slide 4: **Research Questions:** <table><tr><td>Questions</td><td>What are the properties?</td><td>What are examples of uses?</td></tr><tr><td>Rocks</td><td></td><td></td></tr><tr><td>Soil</td><td></td><td></td></tr><tr><td>Water</td><td></td><td></td></tr></table>
Slide 5: **W:** **What do I need to find out the answer to my research question?**	Slide 6: **Information Quest:** **Where can I find information about rocks, soil, and water?**
Slide 7: **L:** **What did I learn from my research?**	Slide 8: **Put it all together** - **Were the questions answered?** - **What would I do differently next time?**

Figure 2.8 Rocks, Soil, and Water PowerPoint®

Session 3

In the classroom, the teacher continues to read aloud information resources and check for comprehension.

Session 4

Meet with the kindergarten teachers and evaluate the product students have presented. Complete the assessment rubric together (Figure 2.9).

Assessment Rubric

SKILL	Level I Minimum	LEVEL II Average	LEVEL III Excellent
Did the student participate in discussion?			
Did the student answer both research questions in the final product?			

Figure 2.9 Rocks, Soil, and Water Assessment Rubric

Resources

If You Find a Rock by Barbara Hirsch Lember

Looking at Rocks (My First Field Guide) by Jennifer Dussling

Experiments with Rocks and Minerals by Salvatore Tocci

Rocks: Hard, Soft, Smooth, and Rough by Natalie M. Rosinsky

Rocks and Fossils (Kingfisher Young Knowledge series) by Chris Pellant

Life in a Bucket of Soil by Alvin and Virginia Silverstein

Soil (*True Books: Natural Resources*) by Christin Ditchfield

Dirt: The Scoop on Soil by Natalie M. Rosinsky

How We Use Soil by Carol Ballard

Soil (First Step Nonfiction: What Earth Is Made ogf) by Robin Nelson

The Magic School Bus Gets Wet All Over: A Book about the Water Cycle by Pat Relf

Follow the Water from Brook to Ocean (Let's-Read-and-Find-Out-Science 2) by Arthur Dorros

Water's Journey by Eleonore Schmid

Did a Dinosaur Drink This Water? by Robert E. Wells

The Drop Goes Plop: A First Look at the Water Cycle by Sam Godwin

It Could Still Be Water by Allan Fowler

14. Let Go My Eco

Grades: 2–8

NATIONAL GEOLOGY STANDARDS			
PLACES AND REGIONS	4		
ENVIRONMENT AND SAFETY	14	15	16
THE USES OF GEOLOGY	18		

Figure 2.10 National Standards for Let Go My Eco

Many areas of the United States face environmental problems and issues. Students can become participants in real world issues by researching and applying knowledge in order to create solutions. Place students into groups (as determined by collaboration with the teachers) to research local ecological issues, such as drought, excessive rainfall, desert conditions, and extreme winters. Devise a plan to help plant and animal life survive. Here is a process for exploring geological issues:

Assess the problem: Survey the local climate and determine ecological problems. Produce a statement or question that deals with the problem. The ultimate goal of this research is to offer a solution proposal.

Information quest: Use the almanac to gain more information on the school's local area. Contact county extension agents in the area. Conduct interviews with local farmers and gardeners. Visit garden shops andvisit with horticultural experts.

Propose a solution: Based on all the information and data gathered from various print and nonprint sources, offer a solution.

Test the solution: In a demonstration garden or a small container garden show the results of the solution proposal.

Assessment Rubric

SKILL	LEVEL I Minimum	LEVEL II Average	LEVEL III Excellent
Did the student groups define the environmental problem accurately?			
Did the student groups follow the AIPT exploration process?			
Is the solution viable and workable?			

Figure 2.11 Let Go My Eco Assessment Rubric

15. Pirate Treasure in the Library

Grades: 3–5

NATIONAL GEOGRAPHY STANDARDS	
The World in Spatial Terms	1: Using Maps

Figure 2.12 National Standards for Pirate Treasure in the Library

Mapping begins with personal space and expands to the world. Discuss with students which buildings or rooms they know very well. Could they draw a map of the room? Tell the students they will be hiding pirate treasure in the library and leave behind a map.

Materials

- White construction paper
- Pencils
- Star stickers
- Red water-based marker

Directions

1. Show students examples of "You Are Here" maps. These types of maps are found in shopping malls and museums. Discuss how the student could find his way to a store in the mall. Use conversation, such as "I would go left at the staircase and then turn right." Stress the importance of using pictures of objects on a map.

2. Break the class into groups of three. Give each group a plastic gold coin and ask the students to hide it somewhere in the library media center.

3. Each group will construct their own maps to locate the treasure. The library circulation desk will be the starting point, so they will mark the desk with a red "X."

4. Student groups trade maps and try to find each others' treasure.

Internet Resources

<www.interactive2.usgs.gov/learningweb/teachers/mapadv_story.htm>

<www.interactive2.usgs.gov/learningweb/teachers/mapadv.htm>

Assessment Rubric

SKILL	LEVEL I Minimum	LEVEL II Average	LEVEL III Excellent
Accuracy of Map?			
Pictorial representation used?			

Figure 2.13 Treasure Map Assessment Rubric

16. Science Camp

Grades: 5–8

Time: One week; one-hour duration

NATIONAL STANDARDS			
National Science Education Standards Science as Inquiry	K-4		5-8
Information Literacy Standards	1	2	3

Figure 2.14 National Standards for Science Camp

Collaborate with teachers to plan a Science Camp to reinforce science concepts before an important (standardized) test. Each person on the team chooses one science concept, and accompanying experiment, that students have difficulty understanding. For one week, the classrooms and the library media center become science laboratories. Students rotate to a different area each day. Excellent resources are available from the AIMS (Activities Integrating Math and Science) Education Foundation™ <www.aimsedu.org/index.html>.

Camp T-shirts can be made easily by asking students or a parent to design a camp logo. The design is printed out and each student is given a copy. With Crayola™ Fabric Crayons, the students color the back, or wrong side, of the printed sheet. Outlining shapes and using a firm touch is recommended. The design is taken home and ironed on to a plain white T-shirt by an adult.

Assessment Rubric

SKILL	LEVEL I Minimum	LEVEL II Average	LEVEL III Excellent
Did the student participate in the experiments and discussion?			
Did the student demonstrate the science concept?			
Was the student able to explain results from the science experiment?			

Figure 2.15 Science Camp Assessment Rubric

17. Science-Telling

All grades

Students participate in science experiments that are incorporated in storytelling events.

NATIONAL SCIENCE EDUCATION STANDARDS			
Content Standard A	K-4		5-8
Content Standard G	1	2	3

Figure 2.16 National Standards for Science-Telling

Story: The Princess and the Boat

Once upon a time a beautiful princess was promised in marriage to a prince. The prince lived on the other side of the river. The day finally came for the princess' wedding. She came to the dock with her maid and her hairdresser.

The captain of the wedding boat greeted her kindly, "Your majesty, all is ready for your departure."

"Thank you, good captain," she responded. The princess was about to board the ship when she noticed that there were lines and numbers on the side of the ship. "Good captain, what is the purpose of these marks?" she asked.

"The numbers show how far the ship is in the water, your majesty," he said as he bowed. "For example, right now you see that the water is right at the line that says number nine. That means that the bottom of the ship is nine feet under the surface of the water."

"Oh, my," said the princess, "I have 10 boxes of gold jewelry to bring aboard the ship. They each weigh exactly the same. Will you be able to safely transport all across the river?" she asked.

The captain replied, "Well, let's see. We will put one in the boat."

They did and now the water was at the line 10. When the captain and the princess climbed aboard, the ship in the water came to 11. The maid and the hairdresser weighed the same as the captain and the princess. The top of the boat had a line that said 18. How many boxes do you think the princess could put on the boat?

Answer: Six more chests will sink the boat.

Supplies

- Large, clear plastic tub
- Medium, clear plastic bowl
- Marker
- Water
- 12 small wooden blocks

Figure 2.17 Materials for the Princess and the Boat

Directions

1. Preparation: Fill the tub with water and mark lines and numbers on the side of the plastic bowl.

2. While telling the story, point out the lines on the bowl and the 12 wooden blocks. Ask a student from the audience to help place the wooden blocks "aboard the boat."

3. After the student has placed three blocks representing the gold jewelry and the people into the boat, pause and ask the audience, "How many boxes do you think the princess could put on the boat?" After several have given an answer, have the volunteer student place the remaining blocks

into the boat.

4. Ask the audience why the boat sunk.

Story: The Dragon is Coming to Town

[In preparation for the story, cover a table and the floor with shower curtains or cut trash bags. Place a bowl on the table.]

The townspeople of Quietville are friendly folk, but value quietness as a great virtue. In fact, everyone whispers all of the time. They greet one another quietly. *[Use a whisper voice while raising a hand in a wave.]*

"Hey there, neighbor!"

The traffic police must never yell.

"Stop! Go!" *[using a whisper voice].*

Quietville's favorite sport is horse racing. However, since the horses must also make no noise, their hoofs are covered with slippers. *[Place house slippers on feet and pretend to run.]* No snoring is allowed in Quietville. *[Snore very quietly.]* One market day, as the townspeople were buying their food for the week, a very loud roar was heard overhead. Startled, the townsfolk looked up and saw a ferocious, fire-breathing dragon.

"I give you two hours to give me all your possessions or I will burn this town and everything in it," screamed the dragon.

With that announcement the dragon turned heel and went up the hill surrounding the town and glared at the townspeople. No one had ever heard anyone or anything speak so loudly, so you can understand their fright. The mayor of Quietville gathered all of the townspeople into the City Hall.

"We must do something quickly!" he said in a strained, yet quiet yell.

"Let's find our own dragon and fight fire with fire," whispered a man.

"They are very noisy and it would be improper for us to use such a creature," voiced the mayor.

All of the townspeople thought and thought.

"I know how to make a quiet, but scary giant," whispered a small child.

"What? You know how to do this? Come forward, young one," said the Mayor. Little Theodora quietly stepped forward.

"How do you propose to make a quiet giant?" asked the mayor.

"All I need is some dish detergent, glycerin, water, and coffee stirrers," said Theodora.

The townsfolk quickly gathered all of the supplies and hurried back to City Hall.

[At this point, choose a girl volunteer.]

Theodora mixed the dish detergent, glycerin, and water in a bowl.

[Help the student mix the items in the bowl.]

"I do need others to help," said Theodora.

[The girl volunteer chooses two more students. Pour a small amount of the bubble solution onto the table and ask the students to blow with coffee stirrers until the table is covered. Students can create arms and a head by placing the coffee stirrer into the solution and blowing while moving away from the solution.]

When the bubble giant was finished the townspeople were astonished. It was quite huge and scary, they thought. At that moment the dragon returned to claim the fortune from the townspeople. When he saw the huge bubble giant and his reflection in each bubble, he gasped in fear and ran far away. He has not been seen or heard from again, which makes the folk of Quietville very happy indeed.

Supplies

- Shower curtains or trash bags cut with scissors to lay flat
- Tape (to tape trash bags together)
- Table
- ¼ cup dish detergent
- 4 tablespoons vegetable glycerin
- 2 cups water
- Small, deep bowl
- Long coffee stirrers

Directions

1. Cover the table and floor with old shower curtains or cut and taped trash bags. Place a small bowl on the table. Choose a volunteer to help mix the glycerin, dish detergent, and water in the bowl. Check the story for the appropriate time.

2. After mixing, ask the student volunteer to choose three more students. Caution the students not to swallow the bubble solution. Using the coffee stirrers with the students, begin to blow bubbles.

Figure 2.18 Bubble Giant

Science Question

- What makes bubbles?

- What can I do to make the bubbles last longer?

- If I change one ingredient in the bubble recipe, does it affect the outcome?

Story: Castle Attack! *[Choose two student volunteers for this story.]*

Supplies

- 1 box of crackers
- 1 jar of creamy peanut butter
- 1 bag of mini-marshmallows
- 2 plastic knives

Once upon a time King Gareth had twin sons. Their names were George and Gregory. As you can see, the king was fond of the letter "G," but that is another story. A feast was prepared for the presentation of the infant princes to their subjects. Their mother, Queen Gwendolyn, proudly carried the two boys into the dining hall.

An old man rose from the crowd and said, "Your majesties, may I offer a word of prophecy?"

Puzzled, the king gave the old man permission to

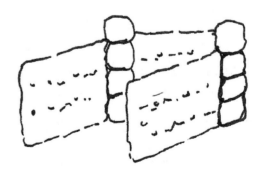

Figure 2.19 Cracker Castle

speak, "Two sons to rule, two sons to war. You, O King, must choose but one."

Astonished, the King and Queen graciously thanked the old man. They pondered the mystery of his words not only at dinner, but over the years. As the two boys grew up, they argued about everything.

"I can run faster than you," said George mockingly to Gregory.

Not to be outdone, Gregory replied, "We'll see about that!"

And off they went, each trying to out run the other until they reached the outer walls of the kingdom. When they were not running, they were competing in horseback riding, skiing, roller skating, skateboarding, reading, writing, math, science, you name it.

"That's it, I have had enough!" yelled the king over dinner, after a particularly bad argument between the brothers over how fast they could eat their peas. "You two must leave the palace and build your own castles," commanded the king. "Whoever builds the strongest castle will rule in my place after I am dead," he said.

So each brother chose a plot of land and gathered his supplies. Prince George constructed his house as such [*Take four bars of graham crackers and help one student place dots of peanut butter along the short edges of each bar. Press the bars together and finish one castle. Set the castle on the paper towel.*]

Prince Gregory decided to create his castle with towers. [*Ask the other student to dot the edges of four more bars of graham crackers, but do not let the student attach the bars to one another. Ask the student to place a dot of peanut butter between each marshmallow and stack up, making one tower. The student takes one bar of graham cracker and attaches the marshmallow tower with the peanut butter on the bar. Attach the next bar to the tower with a peanut butter side.*]

Continue until all towers are in the corners of each bar. Help the students make bridges for the castles by coating one edge of another bar and sticking it to any side of the castles.

Ask the class which castle will stand if an object is run into one corner. (*Answer: The castle with the marshmallows in the corner*). Test the theory out with a finger pressed on the corner of each castle. Why would your choice be the strongest? (*Answer: The marshmallows provide extend support and absorb impact.*) Who received the kingdom? (*Answer: Prince Gregory*)

Assessment Rubric

SKILL	LEVEL I Minimum	LEVEL II Average	LEVEL III Excellent
Listening Skills			
Did the student understand the science concept demonstrated?			
Can the student explain the results of the experiment?			

Figure 2.20 Science-Telling Assessment Rubric

18. Will It Float?

Grades: K–5

NATIONAL SCIENCE EDUCATION STANDARDS		
Physical Science	K-4	5-8

Figure 2.21 National Standards for Will It Float

Columbus Day takes on new meaning when different objects are placed in water. Students will learn about buoyancy as they predict which objects will float or sink.

Supplies

- Small table
- Tub
- Pitcher of water
- Objects to place in water
- Vinyl table cloth or shower curtain

Print Resources

Primary Grades (K – 2)

DK Readers: The Story of Christopher Columbus (Level 2: Beginning to Read) by Mary Ling

History: Hands On: Christopher Columbus by Mary Tucker – This book provides skits, games to discover what motivated Christopher Columbus, food, and rhymes.

Intermediate Grades

Christopher Columbus (History Makers Bios) by Susan Bivin Aller

Christopher Columbus: Sailing to a New World by Adrianna Moganelli

Discovering Christopher Columbus: How History is Invented by Kathy Pelta focuses on controversial moments in Christopher Columbus' life and voyage.

Internet Resources

<www.enchantedlearning.com/explorers/page/c/columbus.html>

The Web site includes information about Christopher Columbus and activities.

<www.castellobanfi.com/features/story_3.html>

A culinary Web site of what the sailors ate on the voyages to the New World.

<www.bbc.co.uk/schools/famouspeople/standard/columbus/index.shtml#focus>

A Web site to learn about Christopher Columbus and take a quiz.

Directions

1. Introduce the new vocabulary words: buoyancy and flotation object. Ask students what they think they mean. Assess prior knowledge.

2. Buoyancy: the ability to rise in a fluid

3. Flotation object: an object that rises in a fluid

4. Introduce the problem: We need to test objects to see which one will make a good flotation object.

5. Place the tub on a small table and cover with a vinyl tablecloth or shower curtain. Fill the tub with the water.

6. Hold up the objects and ask students to make predictions about which will float or sink.

7. After each object, ask why the object floated or why it sank.

8. Ask the students to help create a chart to graph the results.

9. Inquire if there are any new questions raised from the experiment. Challenge students to ask at least two new questions.

Explanation

The science concept being demonstrated is buoyancy. The object placed in the water displaces its volume of water. If an object is lightweight it will float, because it weighs less than the volume of the water. Try comparing a regular can of soda pop with a diet can of soda pop and see what happens. *(The diet soda pop will float because it weighs less than the regular soda pop.)*

Assessment Rubric

SKILL	Level I Minimum	LEVEL II Average	LEVEL III Excellent
Did the student predict what would happen with each object?			
Can the student define buoyancy?			

Figure 2.22 Will It Float? Assessment Rubric

READING INCENTIVE PROGRAM

19. Science Rocks Reading Incentive Program   Grades: 3–8

NATIONAL SCIENCE EDUCATION STANDARDS		
Science in Personal and Social Perspectives	K-4	5-8
History and Nature of Science	K-4	5-8

Figure 2.23 National Standards for Science Rocks Reading Program

Design a reading program based on reading books and magazines with a science focus. The winners will choose an experiment from one of the books and be videotaped (with parental permission)

conducting the experiment. The experiment can be used in the classroom to teach science concepts or be presented as part of the daily student broadcast.

Break the reading requirement into broad science categories:

Physical Science
Light, heat, electricity, and magnetism
Motions and forces
Energy
Conservation of energy
Simple machines
Properties of matter

Science in Personal and Social Perspectives
Personal health
Resources
Changes in environment
Natural hazards
Science and technology in society
Medicine
Anatomy

Earth and Space Science
Earth materials
Objects in the sky
Changes in earth and sky
Earth's history
Earth in the solar system

Life Science
Organisms: animal and plant life
Ecosystems
Habitats
Anatomy

Name: _____   Teacher: _____

Science Rocks Reading Program

Directions: Read at least three books in each category.
      Write the title and two new science facts you learned from the book.

PHYSICAL SCIENCE

1. Title _____

   New Fact _____

   New Fact _____

2. Title _____

   New Fact _____

   New Fact _____

3. Title _____

   New Fact _____

   New Fact _____

Figure 2.24 Science Rocks Reading Log

LIFE SCIENCE

1. Title _____

   New Fact _____

   New Fact _____

2. Title _____

   New Fact _____

   New Fact _____

3. Title _____

   New Fact _____

   New Fact _____

EARTH AND SPACE SCIENCE

1. Title _____

   New Fact _____

   New Fact _____

2. Title _____

   New Fact _____

   New Fact _____

3. Title _____

   New Fact _____

   New Fact _____

Figure 2.24 Science Rocks Reading Log

PERSONAL AND SOCIAL PERSPECTIVES IN SCIENCE

1. Title _____

    New Fact _____

    New Fact _____

2. Title _____

    New Fact _____

    New Fact _____

3. Title _____

    New Fact _____

    New Fact _____

Figure 2.24 Science Rocks Reading Log

Assessment Rubric

SKILL	LEVEL I Minimum	LEVEL II Average	LEVEL III Excellent
Were a variety of science topics read?			
Did the student demonstrate comprehension of the material?			

Figure 2.25 Science Rocks Assessment Rubric

COMMUNITY EVENTS

20. Science Career Day

Grades: 5–8

NATIONAL SCIENCE EDUCATION STANDARDS	
Science in Personal and Social Perspectives	5-8

Figure 2.26 National Standards for Science Career Day

Contact local colleges and universities for science experts who can provide short programs on their field of interest. If no local college exists, a local county extension agent has a wealth of information on soil types, crop growth, and animal husbandry. Parents who work in science fields can add valuable input into a library program on science. Hold a learning center type of experience for students in grades four through eight. Choose three to four science experts in the community and station them in various parts of the library to demonstrate their field or conduct a simple experiment.

21. A Night under the Stars

All grade levels

NATIONAL SCIENCE EDUCATION STANDARDS		
Earth and Space	K-4	5-8

Figure 2.27 National Standards for A Night under the Stars

"A Night under the Stars" is a community-based star gazing party. Solicit support for advertising and organizing the event with parent volunteers or members of the Parent Teacher Association or Parent Teacher Organization. Ask for volunteers to bring telescopes to the school after dark. City lights make viewing difficult, so the sights to be seen will be simple. Star formations, such as the Big Dipper and the Little Dipper, can be seen without the use of a telescope. Use telescopes to view the Moon's surface or other planetary bodies in view during the time of year. Circulate among the groups and observe answers to the following observation objectives.

Observation Objectives

1. Infer that distances in the solar system are great and name the major use of the telescope.

2. Identify the galaxy in which our solar system is located.

3. Identify common constellations, such as the Big Dipper and the Little Dipper. Fall constellations may include Cygnus and Pegasus. Winter constellations may include Taurus and Orion. Spring constellations may include Leo.

Print Resources

Glow-in-the Dark Constellations by C. E. Thompson
Nightwatch: A Practical Guide for Viewing the Universe by Terence Dickinson
Astronomy for All Ages: Discovering the Universe through Activities for Children and Adults
   by Philip Harrington

Internet Resources

<www.stardate.org/nightsky>/

Stardate provides weekly stargazing tips to plan for the next seven days.

<www.wunderground.com/sky/index.asp>

Enter the zip code of the school and find out what stars and constellations can be seen.

<pbskids.org/cyberchase/games/anglemeasurement/anglemeasurement.html>

Cyberchase helps students learn the degrees needed to point a telescope to view planets.

<www.fourmilab.ch/earthview/vplanet.html>

Assessment Rubric

SKILL	LEVEL I Minimum	LEVEL II Average	LEVEL III Excellent
Does the student participate in the star gazing?			
Can the student name the sights seen through the telescope?			

Figure 2.28 A Night under the Stars Assessment Rubric

Chapter 3

OUTRAGEOUS MATH IDEAS

INTRODUCTION

Math strategies and cognition skills play a role in student learning and have a place in the library media center. Including math as collaborative events with classrooms demonstrates the library media center's ability to integrate skills, and plus, it is fun!

COLLABORATION EVENTS

22. Dewey Demystification

Grades: 3–8

STANDARDS FOR SCHOOL MATHEMATICS (National Council of Teachers of Mathematics)
Problem Solving

Figure 3.1 National Standards for Dewey Demystification

Teach place value of the Dewey Decimal Classification System. Discuss what each place value means on a nonfiction book. Coordinate with a decimal lesson in the classroom. Explain that each number relates not only to math, but also to the library. Work in the 700s, a favorite area for many students. Discuss the 900s and their meaning.

Assessment Rubric

SKILL	LEVEL I Minimum	LEVEL II Average	LEVEL III Excellent
Did the student locate non-fiction materials accurately?			

Figure 3.2 Dewey Demystification Assessment Rubric

23. Graph It!

Grades: 3–8

STANDARDS FOR SCHOOL MATHEMATICS (National Council of Teachers of Mathematics)
Data Analysis
Communication

Figure 3.3 National Standards for Graph It!

When classrooms emphasize graphing skills, gather statistical books such as *The Guinness Book of World Records* and almanacs. For example, students gather information about the tallest buildings and create a comparison graph chart.

Assessment Rubric

SKILL	LEVEL I Minimum	LEVEL II Average	LEVEL III Excellent
Did the student represent data accurately?			
Did the student draw conclusions from the data?			

Figure 3.4 Graph it Assessment Rubric

24. The Kids Who Measured the School

Grades: 3–8

STANDARDS FOR SCHOOL MATHEMATICS (National Council of Teachers of Mathematics)
Problem Solving
Connections

Figure 3.5 National Standards for The Kids Who Measured the School

Use *The Librarian Who Measured the Earth* to discuss the historical person, Eratosthenes, Director of The Great Library at Alexandria. His measurements are based on the estimated speed of a caravan of camels. In cooperation with a classroom teacher, decide upon the unit of measure–meters, feet, or an unusual one, such as paper clips. Are students able to estimate the perimeter of the school?

Visit these Web sites to learn more about Eratosthenes and measuring the Earth:

<www.karlscalculus.org/measureearth.html>
<www.algonet.se/~sirius/eaae/aol/market/collabor/erathost/>
<www.physics2005.org/projects/eratosthenes/index.html>

Assessment Rubric

SKILL	LEVEL I Minimum	LEVEL II Average	LEVEL III Excellent
Did the student record information accurately?			
Did the student apply a vairety of strategies to solve the problem?			

Figure 3.6 The Kids Who Measured the School Assessment Rubric

25. Math Around the World

Grades: 2–8

STANDARDS FOR SCHOOL MATHEMATICS (National Council of Teachers of Mathematics)
Problem Solving
Connections

Figure 3.7 National Standards for Math Around the World

Moja – Central Africa

One caller is needed. The caller yells out a number from 1 to 5. One: (moja (MO-jah), Two: mbili (mm-BEE-lee), Three: tatu (TAH-too), Four: nne (NN-nay), and Five: tano (TAH-no.)

Students group themselves into these number groups. If the number two (mbili) is called students group themselves into groups of two.

Wari – Egypt 2 players

Wari is similar to chess. The object of the game is to eliminate the opponent's game pieces. Use two different types of beans for each player; for example, dark red kidney beans and white navy beans. Cut the lid off of a thoroughly cleaned egg carton. On one side of the egg carton one player places four beans into each cup. Keep the lid of the egg carton as a place to put eliminated beans. All playing pieces move to the right.

Fox and Geese – Europe

This game originated in Scandinavia and was called Halatafl. Use buttons, small stones, or beans as playing pieces. A "fox" game piece is placed in the middle of the game board. Thirteen "sheep" line one side of the board. The "sheep" can only move sideways or forward. The "fox" can move in any direction. The "geese" game pieces must force the "fox" into a corner so that he cannot jump and capture any "sheep."

Internet Resources

<www.mastersgames.com/rules/fox-geese-rules.htm>
<www.stoneclave.com/tavern/games/gam_foxgeese.asp>

Great Shopping Site for Games!
<www.greathallgames.com/index.html?main.html>

Print Resources

Math Games and Activities from Around the World and More Math Games and Activities from Around the World by Claudia Zavslasky

Assessment Rubric

SKILL	LEVEL I Minimum	LEVEL II Average	LEVEL III Excellent
Did the student understand the rules of the game?			
Did the student use various strategies to play the game?			

Figure 3.8 Math around the World Assessment Rubric

26. Math Garden

STANDARDS FOR SCHOOL MATHEMATICS (National Council of Teachers of Mathematics)
Measurement
Problem Solving
Communication
Connections

Figure 3.9 National Standards for Math Garden

Put a twist on the traditional garden classroom by creating a Math Garden. Schools with an existing learning garden can jump down to Activities in the Garden for new ideas. Building a garden requires work plus partnership. Seek approval from the principal and think about who is in the learning community–PTA organization, avid gardeners in the neighborhood, or a garden nursery willing to donate supplies. Which grades will be participating in the Math Garden? Older students can help till soil and younger ones can plant seeds. Seek advice from county extension agents or xeriscape experts on what to plant in your school's soil type. Consider the area in which you will plant your garden. Invite students to design the garden plan. Provide research tips on comparison of soils and light.

Many grants are available to help finance a learning garden. Check out these Web sites that help youth gardens:

<www.kidsgardening.com>
<www.garden.org/home>

Activities in the Garden

1. How many square feet is the garden?
2. How many bags of mulch do I need to apply if each bag covers __ square feet?
3. Which plant will take up the most space in my garden?
4. Estimate how much area each plant will cover.
5. Measurement: Students measure the height of plants of the same type. Which one is taller?
6. In the future, if I want to double my yield, how many plants will I need to use?

Assessment Rubric

SKILL	LEVEL I Minimum	LEVEL II Average	LEVEL III Excellent
Did the student employ computation skills accurately in measurement?			
Did the student communicate results effectively?			
Did the student understand the connection between mathematics and real world problems?			

3.10 Math Garden Assessment Rubric

27. Math Magic Bags

Grades: K–8

STANDARDS FOR SCHOOL MATHEMATICS (National Council of Teachers of Mathematics)
Measurement
Problem Solving
Communication
Connections

Figure 3.11 National Standards for Math Magic Bags

Purchase clear backpacks and fill them with a math book and game pieces to play a simple game or learning activity. Students check these out to practice math skills. Align each bag with national or state standards to match up curriculum objectives. Each title listed below has a game or extended questions.

Supplies

Use die-cut box patterns or create a larger box with the following supplies:

- Clear plastic backpacks
- Large ink jet printable labels
- Clear plastic tape
- Game pieces
- Paperback books

Figure 3.12 Photo of Math Magic Bag

Grades K – 2 Book Titles

All Aboard Math Reader Station Stop 3 Breakfast at Danny's Diner: A Book About Multiplication by Judith Stamper
Bart's Amazing Charts by Dianne Ochiltree
Big Bob and the Winter Holiday Potato by Daniel Pinkwater
Busy Bugs: A Book about Patterns by Jayne Harvey
Cat Show by Jayne Harvey
Even Steven and Odd Todd by Kathryn Cristaldi
Go, Fractions! by Judith Stamper
How Much Is that Guinea Pig in the Window? by Joanne Rocklin
Monster Math Picnic by Grace Maccarone
Monster Money by Grace Maccarone
One Hundred Monsters in My School by Bonnie Bader
One Hungry Cat by Joanne Rocklin
Roller Skates! by Stephanie Calmenson

Grades 3 – 8 Book Titles

The Adventures of Penrose the Mathematical Cat by Theoni Pappas
Math Curse by Jon Scieszka
Math Trek: Adventures in the Math Zone by Ivars Peterson and Nancy Henderson
Math Trek 2: A Mathematical Space Odyssey by Ivars Peterson and Nancy Henderson

Mummy Math: An Adventure in Geometry by Cindy Neuschwander
Sir Cumference and the Great Knight of Angleland: A Math Adventure by Cindy Neuschwander
Sir Cumference and the Sword in the Cone: A Math Adventure by Cindy Neuschwander
What's Your Angle, Pythagoras? by Julie Ellis

Books to Use to Create Games

The Everything Kids' Math Puzzles Book: Brain Teasers, Games, and Activities for Hours of Fun by Meg Clemens, Sean Glenn, Glenn Clemens, and Sean Clemens

Games for Math by Peggy Kaye

Instant File-Folder Games for Math (Grades 1–3) by Linda Ward Beech

Janice VanCleave's Geometry for Every Kid: Easy Activities that Make Learning Geometry by Janice VanCleave

Games can be placed in a Math Magic Bag or paired with a book, such as the game Payday by Winning Moves and the picture book *Alexander Who Used to Be Rich Last Sunday* by Judith Viorst.

3-in-1 Math Readiness Grades PK-2 by Educational Insights

3-in-1 Math Intermediate Grade 3 and Up by Educational Insights

Factor Frenzy by Learning Resources

Fractions Game by Creative Toys USA

Assessment Rubric

SKILL	LEVEL I Minimum	LEVEL II Average	LEVEL III Excellent
Did the student use strategies to solve problems?			
Does the student connect the mathematical problem solving to real world situations?			

Figure 3.13 Math Magic Bags Assessment Rubric

28. Percentage Quest

Grades: 3–8

STANDARDS FOR SCHOOL MATHEMATICS (National Council of Teachers of Mathematics)
Number and Operations
Problem Solving
Connections

Figure 3.14 National Standards for Percentage Quest

Ask students to calculate the percentage of biographies about women in the library. Take an average of three shelves and compare results. Challenge students to recommend titles to boost collection development in the selected area.

75 Outrageous Ways for Librarians to Impact Student Achievement in Grades K – 8

Assessment Rubric

SKILL	LEVEL I Minimum	LEVEL II Average	LEVEL III Excellent
Did the student use computation skills accurately?			
Did the student apply the math concept to a real world problem?			

Figure 3.15 Percentage Quest Assessment Rubric

29. Poster Math

Grades: K–8

STANDARDS FOR SCHOOL MATHEMATICS (National Council of Teachers of Mathematics)
Measurement Standard
Problem Solving
Communication
Connections

Figure 3.16 National Standards for Poster Math

Use leftover posters from book fairs to create math centers in collaboration with teachers. Ask teachers for input into the type of mathematical problems students seem to having difficulty with. The following are examples for fifth grade.

Car Poster

Michael drove his Lotus Elise™ 6,000 meters to Jose's house. Together, Michael and Jose drove 9,000 meters to school. What is the number of kilometers that Michael drove his car?

Adorable Kitties Poster

It takes two gallons of milk to feed five kittens each week. A gallon contains about 3,785 milliliters. How many liters does each kitten drink?

Flying Jets Poster

Antonio flies 9.9 miles on Mondays. He flies 7.6 miles Tuesdays through Fridays. How many miles does Antonio fly in two weeks?

Assessment Rubric

SKILL	LEVEL I Minimum	LEVEL II Average	LEVEL III Excellent
Did the student perform number operations correctly?			
Did the student apply a variety of strategies to solve the problem?			
Did the student connect the mathematical exercise with real world problems?			

Figure 3.17 Poster Math Assessment Rubric

COMMUNITY EVENTS: MATH LEARNING CENTERS   Grades: PK–5

Create learning centers with teachers in the library media center based on math books during National Math Month in April. Invite parents to an evening event to play math games with their children.

PRINCIPALS AND STANDARDS FOR SCHOOL MATHEMATICS (National Council of Teachers of Mathematics)
Measurement
Algebra
Communication
Connections

Figure 3.18 National Standards for Math Learning Centers

30. Number Collage   Grades: PK–1

Goal: to create a picture of one number

Materials

Use die-cut box patterns or create a larger box with the following supplies:

- Old magazines and newspapers
- Scissors
- Glue
- Construction paper

Directions

Choose a number from 1 to 10. Look through the magazines and newspapers to find several pictures of the number. Cut each out and glue to the paper.

75 Outrageous Ways for Librarians to Impact Student Achievement in Grades K – 8

31. Fruit Loop® Math

Grades: PK–1

Goal: to graph the colors of the cereal

Materials

- Fruit Loop® cereal placed in snack bags
- Graph Chart

Directions

Teacher: Preparing the graph sheet

1. Using a sheet of white 8 1/2 x 11 inch paper, placed in the landscape position, make marks across the top of the sheet with colored markers representing the colors of Fruit Loops®.

2. Use a black marker to make lines seperating the colors.

Look at the colors at the top of each line on the graph chart. Find the color in the bag and place it under the color at the bottom of the row. Which color has the most loops? Which color has the fewest?

32. Egg Math

All grades

Goal: solve the mathematical equations

Materials

- 1 clean egg carton
- 12 plastic eggs with math problems written on each
- Snack size plastic bags
- Split peas
- Paper

Buy plastic Easter eggs on sale after Easter for this math game. Write math problems on each egg. This activity can be adapted for all grade levels.

Directions

Pick an egg. Work the math problem on paper. Place the number of peas into the egg that solves the math problem.

33. Calculator Activity

All grades

Goal: use simple or more difficult directions to solve problems

34. Biggest and Smallest

Grades: 2–3

Goal: to make the highest score

Materials

- Pencil

- Paper
- 2 die

Directions

Player one takes the two die and rolls them on the table. Use the numbers on top of the die to make the biggest two-digit number. Write the number on a sheet of paper. Throw the die again. This time make the smallest two-digit number possible. If the second number is bigger than the first, throw the die again. When you have a smaller number write it below the first number on the paper. Subtract the bottom number from the top. The answer is the score. Write it on the sheet of paper. The next player takes a turn. Keep going around the group until everyone has had a chance. When everyone has made a bigger and smaller number, the first player plays again. The first person to receive a 100 wins the game.

Example: 64 – 25 = 39. Score: 39

35. The Big Tree

Grades: 2–5

Goal: to find out how tall this plant will be when it is six years old

Materials

- One plant
- Rulers
- Paper
- Pencil

Directions

The plant on the table grew this tall in one year. Determine how tall the plant will be when it is six years old. Write your answer on a slip of paper.

36. Book Measuring

Grades: 1–5

Goal: to measure the perimeter of a table

Materials

- Student dictionary
- Paper
- Pencil

Directions

Use the book on the table to measure the perimeter of the tabletop. If you do not know what perimeter means, the book on the table is a dictionary. Look up "perimeter".

37. Tangram Activity

Grades: 2–5

Goal: to make a simple shape

Materials

- Tangram pieces

Directions

Place one set of tangram pieces into various shapes. Find tangram shapes at <http://windbagandthunder.blogspot.com/2006/06/more-tangram-designs.html>.

38. Story Problem Challenge

Grades: 2–5

Write a number sentence based on learning objectives in the classroom. Students will write a story to go with the problem.

> **For example:** $24 \div 4 = 6$

Materials

- Index cards with the number sentence written on the blank side
- Pencils

Directions

Write a story problem on the back of the index card that matches the number sentence on the front of the card.

39. Shop Until You Drop

Grades: 3–5

Goal: to shop without going over the $250 budget

Materials

- Calculator
- Flyers from stores
- Pencil
- Paper

Directions

The budget for shopping at this store is $250. Calculate the amount purchased without going over the budgeted amount. Be sure to include state tax. (Note: insert the state tax percentage.) How much money is left? How many items were you able to purchase? For more activities, including interactive games, try this Web site:

> <www.eduplace.com/monthlytheme/april/math_activities.html>

Assessment Rubric for all Math Centers

SKILL	LEVEL I Minimum	LEVEL II Average	LEVEL III Excellent
Does the student use a variety of strategies to solve problems?			
Does the student demonstrate accuracy?			

Figure 3.19 Math Learning Centers Assessment Rubric

Chapter 4

OUTRAGEOUS IDEAS for MUSIC, VISUAL ARTS, & THEATRE

INTRODUCTION

The arts enhance every curriculum area in the school, yet often they are relegated to 30 minutes of instruction, or not at all. Arts integration can be used to reach disenfranchised students and inspire teachers (Werner and Freeman, 2001). Simply put, the arts engage students and their teachers in learning. Collaborating with the music, art, and drama department in the school can yield very creative results as well as aid in the connection between external concepts and integrated knowledge.

40. Artful Learning Ideas

Grades: K–8

NATIONAL STANDARDS for ARTS EDUCATION
Visual Arts
Content Standard 6
Music:
Content Standard 8
Theatre:
Content Standard 2

Figure 4.1 National Standards for Artful Learning Ideas

- Read a story or an article to students and ask them to draw a picture of its meaning.
- Act out new vocabulary words.
- Beat a drum while reading rhythmic poetry.
- Draw results from science experiments.
- Create a visual representation of math concepts. Visit <mathforum.org/~sarah/shapiro/> for ideas to connect drawing to geometry.
- Artists are storytellers. Ask students to describe the plot, characters, and setting in paintings.

Assessment Rubric

SKILL	LEVEL I Minimum	LEVEL II Average	LEVEL III Excellent
Theater: Can the student effectively improvise actions for vocabulary words?			
Does the student understand the relationship between visual arts/music/theater and other curriculum areas?			
Music: Does the student appreciate the connection between music and different cultures?			

Figure 4.2 Artful Ideas Assessment Rubric

41. Get Graphic!

Grades: 5–8

NATIONAL STANDARDS FOR ARTS EDUCATION
Visual Arts
Content Standard 1

Figure 4.3 National Standards for Get Graphic

Book talk graphic novels. Invite local high school art students to demonstrate their drawing technique and discuss story structure. Set up a graphic writing and drawing center in the library.

Print Resources

Draw Manga: How to Draw Manga In Your Own Unique Style by Bruce Lewis
Draw Your Own Manga: All the Basics by Haruno Nagatomo
How to Draw Manga by Katy Coope
Manga Mania: How to Draw Japanese Comics by Christopher Hart–reviewed by School Library Journal
Manga Mania Fantasy Worlds: How to Draw the Enchanted Worlds of Japanese Comics by Christopher Hart

Assessment Rubric

SKILL	LEVEL I Minimum	LEVEL II Average	LEVEL III Excellent
Does the student use media safely?			
Does the student use the media to tell a story?			

Figure 4.4 Get Graphic! Assessment Rubric

42. Music Connection

Grades: K–8

NATIONAL STANDARDS for ARTS EDUCATION
Music:
Content Standard 8

Figure 4.5 National Standards for Music Connection

Purchase instruments from around the world, such as a thumb piano, castanets, Brazilian Caxixi, chimes, cymbals, tambourines, drums, and gongs. Demonstrate playing instructions to students prior to reading or storytelling, for accompaniment.

The NIU World Music Instrument Collection site allows the user to click on a region then hear the sound of an instrument.

<www.engineering.usu.edu/ece/faculty/wheeler/NIU/index.htm>

Sources for Purchase

World Musical Instruments.Com: <www.worldmusicalinstruments.com/default.asp>

Sunreed Instruments:

Lark in the Morning: <larkinthemorning.com/Default.asp?bhcd2=1173884448>

Assessment Rubric

SKILL	Level I Minimum	LEVEL II Average	LEVEL III Excellent
Does the student appreciate the connection between music and different cultures?			
Does the student use the media to tell a story?			

Figure 4.6 Music Connection Assessment Rubric

43. Picture Book Artists

Grades: K–8

NATIONAL STANDARDS FOR ARTS EDUCATION
Visual Arts
Content Standard 1

Figure 4.7 National Standards for Picture Book Artists

Take an online tour of art from The National Center for Children's Illustrated Literature Museum <www.nccil.org> in Abilene, Texas. The museum has created art projects to match picture books <www.nccil.org/activities.html>. These ideas can be used in collaborations with the art teacher. Read the book featured in the art project and accurately describe the illustrator's style.

In preparation for a collaborative unit, talk about the history of picture books, beginning with Randolph Caldecott, a nineteenth century illustrator. He is thought to be the first artist to illustrate children's books. A thorough biography, complete with Caldecott's art work, can be found at <www.randolphcaldecott.org.uk/who.htm>.

Assessment Rubric

SKILL	LEVEL I Minimum	LEVEL II Average	LEVEL III Excellent
Did the student show understanding of the concept by developing a visual response?			
Did the student explore varied ways to express the content of the activity?			
Did the student use the vocabulary of art in describing his or her work?			

Figure 4.8 Picture Book Artists Assessment Rubric

44. Readers Theater Scripts

Grades: K–8

NATIONAL STANDARDS FOR ARTS EDUCATION
Theatre:
Content Standard 1
Content Standard 2

Figure 4.9 National Standards for Readers Theater Scripts

Many resources are available to enrich reading and comprehension by collaborating with the drama teacher. The drama teacher can supply instruction in script writing, dialogue style, and movement. All combined, a visual, memorable experience is created. Many scripts are available online to teach science concepts, such as the water cycle. Paired with a nonfiction resource, concepts become tangible.

Online and Print Resources

For Teachers

<www.loiswalker.com/catalog/teach.htm>l

Grades K – 3

25 Just-Right Plays For Emergent Readers by Carol Pugliano-Martin
Readers Theater Grade 1 – 5 published by Evan-Moor
<www.teachingheart.net/readerstheater.htm>
<www.readerstheatre.ecsd.net/collection.htm>

Grades 3 – 5

Readers Theater for Building Fluency: Strategies and Scripts for Making the Most of This Highly Effective, Motivating, and Research-Based Approach to Oral Reading by Jo Worthy
Readers' Theater Grade 5: Science and Social Studies published by Steck Vaughn

Grades 6 – 8

Readers Theatre Strategies in the Middle and Junior High Classroom: A Take Part Teacher's Guide: Springboards to Language Development Through Readers Theatre, Storytelling, Writing, and Dramatizing by Lois Walker
Readers' Theater, Grade 6 by Michael Ryall
Reader's Theater Scripts – Secondary by M.S.T. Gail Skroback Hennessey

Assessment Rubric

SKILL	LEVEL I Minimum	LEVEL II Average	LEVEL III Excellent
Can the student effectively improvise voice and actions for script?			
Is the student's voice clear and voluble for the audience to hear?			

Figure 4.10 Readers Theater Script Assessment Rubric

45. Artists Helping Children

Grades: K–8

Artists Helping Children, part of The National Heritage Foundation, has many opportunities for children to help terminally ill children in the hospital or at home. They can make pictures or cards, paint tote bags, paint pre-drawn canvases to be sent to the hospital or home of a terminally ill child, and many more ideas available at the group's Web site

<www.artistshelpingchildren.org/wayschildrencanvolunteer.html>

The group also needs donations of old and new art supplies.

Chapter 5

OUTRAGEOUS IDEAS for SOCIAL STUDIES

INTRODUCTION

As with any curriculum area, the outrageous librarian wants to immerse students to foster a deeper understanding of the subject. True learning in social studies does not happen with rote memorization of dates of battles and rulers of lands. True learning happens when students are involved in the cultural, social, and political nature of historical periods and geographical entities. From these experiences, students can create pathways of knowledge based on the study of cultural and social aspects of history and society.

COLLABORATION EVENTS

46. Connect with the World   Grades: 4–8

NATIONAL COUNCIL FOR THE SOCIAL STUDIES
CURRICULUM STANDARDS FOR THE SOCIAL STUDIES
IV

Figure 5.1 National Standards for Connect with the World

Partnership that goes beyond the ordinary boundaries of the school and communicates globally greatly impacts students and the library media center program. The "outrageous" librarian shares the school's curriculum with other schools around the world to impact student learning. An example can be found at <http://209.184.141.5/deepwood/library_files/What%20Does%20Peace%20Feel%20Like1.pps>

Preliminary Steps for the Library Media Specialist

Contact the International Library Association <www.iasl-slo.org> to gather names of library media specialists who would be willing to conduct a book study with their students. Click on "About IASL" to find a list of e-mail addresses for regional directors. Choose a continent and inquire about collaboration projects. Select the language of the collaborating school.

An excellent choice for a book study is *What Does Peace Feel Like* by Vladimir Radunsky. It describes in concrete, kid-friendly terms what the word peace means to students in Italy and the United States. Students created the definitions and Vladimir Radunsky illustrated each in the book. Also, poetry studies work well. For example, for Caribbean students, select *A Caribbean Dozen: Poems from the Caribbean Poets*. Choose *Laughing Tomatoes and Other Spring Poems/Jitomates Resuenos y Otras Poemas* de *Primavera* by Francisco X. Alarcon.

Once contact has been made with the collaborating librarian, a decision can be made about the format of communication–e-mail, air mail, a PowerPoint™ presentation, or a Web page. Each school purchases the book to be studied. If the collaborating school cannot afford the book, purchase the book for the school and ship it.

Lesson Plan: (4 sessions)

This plan is flexible. Use this project with an entire grade level or just a few classes.

Session 1

Using a world map, show students the country and location of the collaborating international school. Read about the country from nonfiction books or reference books. Classroom teachers can tie this unit in with units in social studies and language arts by collaborating with the LMS in a research project.

After reading the selected book, challenge students to write poetry to the students in the international school. Illustrations are not required, but are desirable. Students should sign only their first name to their project.

Session 2

Students create poetry and illustrations on paper.

Session 3

After the poetry is collected, receive permission from the parents to e-mail, videotape, or post poems on a Web page. Students help scan the artwork and create the PowerPoint™ presentation.

Session 4

Conduct a reading or viewing if students in the cooperating schools have the technology to transmit video clips.

Assessment Rubric

SKILL	LEVEL I Minimum	LEVEL II Average	LEVEL III Excellent
Does the student's work explore and express an understanding of the word peace?			
Is the student's representative work clear and concrete?			

Figure 5.2 Connect with the World Assessment Rubric

47. Guinness Gotcha Game

Grades: 4–8

Combine weird facts with index and keyword usage in this fun game.

NATIONAL COUNCIL FOR THE SOCIAL STUDIES
CURRICULUM STANDARDS FOR THE SOCIAL STUDIES
III

NATIONAL COUNCIL OF TEACHERS OF ENGLISH			
STANDARDS FOR THE ENGLISH LANGUAGE ARTS		6	

Figure 5.3 National Standards for Guinness Gotcha Game

75 Outrageous Ways for Librarians to Impact Student Achievement in Grades K – 8

Materials

- White construction paper
- 4 – 6 copies of *The Guinness Book of World Records* from the same year
- Chart paper or white board
- Marker or dry-erase marker

Directions

Preparation

Teacher and Library Media Specialist: Prepare 20 questions before the lesson begins. Choose two or three questions from each section: Planet Earth, Life on Earth, Human Body, Human Achievements, Society, Science and Technology, Arts and Media, Engineering, and Sports and Games. Possible questions include:

- Where are the world's largest forested areas?
- Name the largest active volcano.
- Where is the driest place in the world?
- How is the flying frog able to glide almost 50 feet?
- What is the name of the fish with the greatest sense of smell?
- What is the most urgent health problem in the world?
- Who ate the most chili peppers in one minute?
- What is the greatest height that an egg has been dropped and remained in one piece?
- Who had the greatest number of soccer goals?
- Who received the largest advance for a nonfiction book?
- What are the dimensions of the world's largest pop-up book?
- Who is the oldest author to have a first book published?
- What is the name of the first movie filmed in Hollywood?

Place students at tables with one copy of *The Guinness Book of World Records* of the same year at each table. Make sure an equal number of students are placed at each table.

On chart paper or white board, denote the teams with a corresponding number or letter.

Playing the Game

One person at each table receives a copy of the book and holds it in the air. After the question is read, the students work as a team to use their knowledge of index organization and keyword structure to search for the answer to the question.

One group member is chosen to give the correct answer, stands up, and responds with the page number and the answer. The teacher/librarian notes the team's win with a mark. The book is passed to another person at the table, and the game proceeds. The first team to finish, using each person at the table, is declared the winner.

Assessment Rubric

SKILL	Level I Minimum	LEVEL II Average	LEVEL III Excellent
Does the student group use accurate location skills?			
Is teamwork evident?			

Figure 5.4 Guinness Gotcha Assessment Rubric

48. Kamishibai Stories

All grades

NATIONAL COUNCIL FOR SOCIAL STUDIES AND CURRICULUM STANDARDS FOR SOCIAL STUDIES
I

Figure 5.5 National Standards for Kamishibai Stories

Kamishibai is a storytelling method that originated in Japan in the 1920s. Kamishibai storytellers traveled from village to village on bicycles with a Kamishibai stage and stories on the back. The storyteller would clap two solid blocks of wood (hyoshigi) together to gather neighborhood children to listen to stories on thick cards. To purchase Kamishibai stories, hyoshigi, and a stage, visit <kamishibai.com>. Each mesmerizing story has a theme, such as personal responsibility, importance of work, unselfishness, and compassion, just to name a few.

Extension Activity

Grades: 4+

- Read *Kamishibai Man* by Allen Say to provide background information.
- Tell a Kamishibai story.
- Ask students to compose their own story cards in small groups.
- After the writing and drawing of cards, have students perform and critique voice quality.
- Later, students present their Kamishibai stories to the younger grade levels or a nearby elementary school.

Assessment Rubric

SKILL	LEVEL I Minimum	LEVEL II Average	LEVEL III Excellent
Is the student able to state the meaning of the story?			
Does the student-produced Kamishibai story meld drawings with story plot?			

Figure 5.6 Kamishibai Stories Assessment Rubric

49. Living Wax Museum

Grades: 4–8

NATIONAL COUNCIL FOR SOCIAL STUDIES AND CURRICULUM STANDARDS FOR SOCIAL STUDIES
III
National Standards for Arts Education
Theater: Content Standards 2 and 5
ALA Information Literacy Standards
All Standards

Figure 5.7 National Standards for the Living Wax Museum

Hill Country Middle School (Eanes Independent School District, Austin, Texas) Physical Education Teacher, Sherrill Barron, creates a Living Wax Museum in cooperation with the library media specialist and drama teacher, thus combining several curriculum areas. In the library, research begins with student selection of a famous person. The culmination of the project is the student performance as the famous person on which the research is conducted. The librarian instructs students on the research process using graphic organizers, such as the ones found at <www.readwritethink.org/lesson_images/lesson243/web.pdf> which help to summarize and map the contributions of the famous person's life. The physical education teacher instructs students on movement and balance. The drama teacher coaches students on the action poses, expression, and speech. Once the student has completed the research and instruction in drama and physical education, a day is chosen for the Living Wax Museum. The gymnasium is used and students enter by classes. The student exhibits perform a simple action related to the famous person when the class passes by. For example, "Tiger Woods" swings an imaginary golf club. "Marian Anderson," a famous African-American opera singer, mimes a song. Students stop at exhibits and ask the "famous person" to tell about themselves. The "famous person" includes important details about his or her life and contributions to history.

Assessment Rubric

SKILL	LEVEL I Minimum	LEVEL II Average	LEVEL III Excellent
Is the student able to conduct research using synthesis and evaluation?			
Does the student display proper body movement for the famous person?			
Does the student summarize major contributions and facts of the famous person?			

Figure 5.8 Living Wax Museum Assessment Rubric

50. Odd Inventions

Grades: K–8

NATIONAL COUNCIL FOR SOCIAL STUDIES AND CURRICULUM STANDARDS FOR SOCIAL STUDIES
VIII

Figure 5.9 National Standards for Odd Inventions

Spark interest in past inventions by injecting humor with a study of some of the weirdest inventions ever. Listed below are Web sites that compile many odd inventions:

<brucevanpatter.com/strangeinventions.html>
<incrediblystrange.com/inventions/index.html>
<delphion.com/gallery>

After viewing the inventions, challenge students to create their own. By Kids for Kids conducts competitions for students. Information and winners are available at <www.bkfk.com/>. Famous inventors and inventions can be studied at the Web site, in addition to tutorials to learn how to invent.

 Assessment Rubric

SKILL	LEVEL I Minimum	LEVEL II Average	LEVEL III Excellent
Did the students address the basic purpose of their invention?			
Did the student groups create an invention via a process of brainstorming, postulation, and peer review?			

Figure 5.10 Odd Inventions Assessment Rubric

COMMUNITY EVENTS

51. World Cultures Night

All grades

NATIONAL COUNCIL FOR THE SOCIAL STUDIES CURRICULUM STANDARDS FOR SOCIAL STUDIES
VIII

Figure 5.11 National Standards for World Cultures Night

Team with classroom, art, music, and drama teachers to plan a family event for the entire community to appreciate and learn about world cultures. Set up booths around the school featuring different regions, such as Mexico, India, Africa, Europe, and China. Solicit parents with backgrounds in these regions to loan and present cultural highlights. Work with the music and drama teacher to plan a special event to end the night with singing and dancing.

52. Adopt a School in Africa

Grades: K–8

NATIONAL COUNCIL FOR THE SOCIAL STUDIES CURRICULUM STANDARDS FOR SOCIAL STUDIES
III

Figure 5.12 National Standards for Adopt a School in Africa

Trudy Marshall, a library media specialist in Round Rock, Texas, formed Libraries of Love <www.librariesoflove.org>, a nonprofit group that builds libraries in Africa. Libraries are built in Uganda schools with no existing library. The Web site contains a map and facts about Uganda to use with classes. A deeper

75 Outrageous Ways for Librarians to Impact Student Achievement in Grades K – 8

study will lead to student discovery of the societal and cultural reasons for the state of affairs in Africa.

Libraries of Love team members bring materials to build shelves, set up computer centers, and catalog and shelve donated books. To help donate materials, set up a large box outside or inside the library during book fairs and holidays for students to donate gently used paperbacks. Students can create bookmarks to send to African children. Checks, bookmarks, or book donations can be sent to: Libraries of Love, 104 Elm Drive, Pflugerville, Texas 78660.

53. The Mercy Corps and The Hunger Site   Grades: PK–8

These two sites have teamed together to create teacher resources available at <www.greatergood.com/newsroom/ths/FamilyHomePage.html>. The site has an elementary curriculum, activities, country studies, and games.

NATIONAL COUNCIL FOR SOCIAL STUDIES AND CURRICULUM STANDARDS FOR SOCIAL STUDIES
X

Figure 5.13 National Standards for The Mercy Corps and The Hunger Site

Suggestions for school and community involvement include selling tickets to a hunger banquet. To illustrate the inequalities of food access for many people in the world, the majority of participants are served a bowl of rice, some are served a modest meal, and a very few number are served a full banquet meal. Students can also create and sell cards, posters, art, or ornaments that contain messages of peace. Communities can also have unusual marathons, such as a poem-a-thon and a picture-a-thon. Each participant seeks support for each poem written or each picture drawn.

54. Save the Children   Grades: PK–8

This site sponsors programs to benefit poverty-stricken children in the United States and the around the world. The group sponsors an art contest with a $500 savings bond award for the winner. Details can be found at <www.savethechildren.org/corporate/art_contest.asp>.

For National Standards, see Figure 5.12.

Chapter 6

OUTRAGEOUS IDEAS in TECHNOLOGY

INTRODUCTION

"Outrageous" library media specialists play a huge role in the technological preparation of students. Consider all the equipment available in the media center. In what other room will you find such variety of equipment? Whether it is very basic or very high-tech, the equipment available can foster creative projects with classroom teachers.

55. Broadcast News!   Grades: 4–8

ISTE (INTERNATIONAL SOCIETY FOR TECHNOLOGY IN EDUCATION) NATIONAL EDUCATION TECHNOLOGY STANDARDS FOR STUDENTS
Content Standard IV

Figure 6.1 National Standards for Broadcast News!

Involve students in the daily announcements by creating a broadcast news service. This can be done at a very basic level. Below is a list of equipment needed for a low dollar investment. However, a classroom cable connection is essential.

Basic Equipment

- Long table
- Chairs
- Used computer–try looking at thrift shops
- Table microphone
- VCR
- Digital video camera

Additional Equipment for an Upgraded Broadcast

- 2–3 stage lights
- 2 lapel microphones
- 1 omni microphone
- Laptop computer
- Video board–for camera transitions, background
- VCR/DVD player recorder
- 13" television
- Teleprompter
- 2 digital video cameras

Writing the Broadcast

Students write the daily broadcast on Microsoft PowerPoint™ or on the teleprompter. Several items can be included in a daily broadcast:

- School menu
- Weather forecast
- Pledge
- This Day in History: <www.history.com/tdih.do> – Video content, but has commercials, <www.infoplease.com/dayinhistory>
- Math Problem of the Day or Week–when working with multiple grades, create one problem, such as for the primary grades, and a higher level problem for intermediate grades.
- Poem of the Day or Week
- Student Work–students read or contribute artwork or photographs to be shown on the broadcast.
- Science Experiment of the Week – choose simple experiments to conduct on-camera. If possible, film ahead and replay during the morning broadcast.

Sample Broadcast

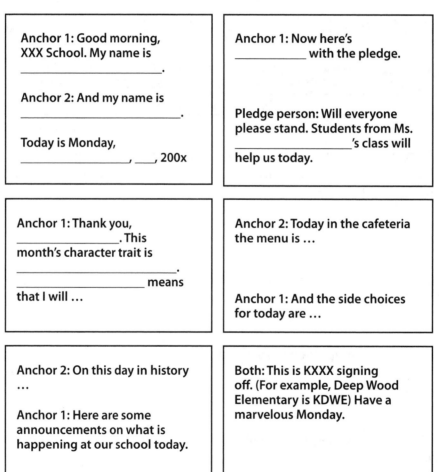

Anchor 1: Good morning, XXX School. My name is
_____.

Anchor 2: And my name is
_____.

Today is Monday,
_____, ____, 200x

Anchor 1: Now here's
_____ with the pledge.

Pledge person: Will everyone please stand. Students from Ms. _____'s class will help us today.

Anchor 1: Thank you,
_____. This month's character trait is
_____.
_____ means that I will …

Anchor 2: Today in the cafeteria the menu is …

Anchor 1: And the side choices for today are …

Anchor 2: On this day in history …

Anchor 1: Here are some announcements on what is happening at our school today.

Both: This is KXXX signing off. (For example, Deep Wood Elementary is KDWE) Have a marvelous Monday.

Figure 6.2 Sample Broadcast Script

Writing a Broadcast

First, choose students for the positions listed below:

- Anchor 1
- Anchor 2
- Reporter 1
- Reporter 2
- Teleprompter
- Video Board
- Sound Technician
- Director

Some schools use upperclassmen for selection. Develop a résumé that can be submitted for consideration by the library media staff. See the sample in Figure 6.3.

Student Resume

Name: _____

Job desired: _____

Experience: (Include any previous experience with a camera, computers, or speaking parts; any jobs you have completed at home or at school; or any awards received)

Qualifications: (Tell why you would like the position, and/or list your character qualities, such as responsible, hard worker, etc.)

Please note: Admission on the broadcast team is pending your teacher's approval.

Figure 6.3 Student Resume Form

Assessment Rubric

SKILL	LEVEL I Minimum	LEVEL II Average	LEVEL III Excellent
Did the students include all facts and announcements in the written broadcast?			
Did the students speak clearly, enunciate words, and use expression in their voice and features?			
Did the students at the camera, video board, and teleprompter perform quickly and responsively?			

Figure 6.4 Broadcast News! Assessment Rubric

56. Create an ezine

Grades: 5–8

ISTE (International Society for Technology in Education) National Education Technology Standards for Students
Content Standard 4

Figure 6.5 National Standards for ezine

An ezine (pronounced 'ee-zeen') is an electronic magazine that can be emailed or posted on a Web site. Most simple ezines are purely text with no interactive elements. This collaborative tool can be used with classroom or school news. It is necessary to have a text editor, such as Microsoft FrontPage.®

Session 1: Format Decisions

Bring in examples of print newsletters or explore on the Web for ezines. The masthead is the title of the ezine and a graphic can be included. The issue number and date are listed below the masthead. For a sample masthead, see Figure 6.6. Invite students to create masthead designs.

THE ELEMENTARY NEWS

Vol. 1, No. 1   September, 2008

Figure 6.6 ezine Masthead Sample

Session 2: Vote on the Masthead

The class votes on the masthead for the ezine. Next, choose the number of columns. Keep the format to one or two columns, for easy readability.

Session 3 – 7: (4 sessions) Choose the Monthly or Semester Staff

Required staff members include the production director, reporters, photographers, proofreaders, and art director. The production editor and the teacher review classroom projects and school news and choose items to report. In addition, the production editor keeps the ezine on task and monitors the work. The reporters and photographers interview, write, and edit news items. All material should be typed and saved into the student's folder on a computer. The proofreaders examine all written articles for grammatical and spelling errors. The classroom teacher and/or library media specialist are the editors-in-chief. They review all items and check for permission to use any photographs of students before submitting the material to the principal for final approval. In particular, the editors-in-chief avoid using students' last names.

Session 8: Build the ezine

Reporters open their files and drop the information into the created template. A sample template can be viewed in Figure 6.7. The art director and the production editor check for presentation quality.

MASTHEAD		
TABLE OF CONTENTS		
☐ Article 1		
☐ Article 2		
☐ Article 3		
Article 1		
Article 2		
Article 3		
Signature		

Figure 6.7 ezine Template

Session 9: Send the ezine

The ezine is sent to parents' email addresses, if permission has been granted. Parental permission must also be secured if the ezine is posted on the school Web site.

Assessment Rubric

SKILL	LEVEL I Minimum	LEVEL II Average	LEVEL III Excellent
Student participation: Did students in the group perform their functions?			
Are all elements of an ezine, or newsletter, present?			
Are technology tools used effectively to communicate with the learning community?			

Figure 6.8 ezine Assessment Rubric

57. Connected Tech

http://corporate.classroom.com/about.html

ISTE (International Society for Technology in Education) National Education Technology Standards for Teachers
Content Standard III

Figure 6.9 National Standards for Teachers of Connected Tech

Connected Tech offers technology enriched lesson plans, tutorials, projects, and assessments for teachers. The material is arranged by grade level and curriculum area. Each area addresses the ISTE National Educational Technology Standards (NETS) for students. Within the teacher resources section, Connected Tech offers 450 lessons, 2,000 software tutorials, 11,000 Web links, and 170 rubrics, quizzes, and assessments.

58. Smart Board® Ideas

Grades: 2–8

ISTE (International Society for Technology in Education) National Education Technology Standards for Teachers
Content Standard III

Figure 6.10 National Standards for Teachers of Smart Board® Ideas

Grab students' attention when presenting research and skills sessions.

For a tutorial on how to use the Smart Board® and its special features, visit the Smart Technologies™ Web site at <www.smarttech.com/trainingcenter/material.asp>.

For ideas in many curriculum areas, try these Web sites:

<http://schoolweb.missouri.edu/morganr2.k12.mo.us/resources/smartboard.htm>
<http://eduscapes.com/sessions/smartboard/>
<www.center.k12.mo.us/edtech/SB/SB.html>
<http://topmarks.co.uk/Interactive.aspx>
<www.center.k12.mo.us/edtech/SB/SITemplates.htm>

For library media center orientation sessions, create a Microsoft PowerPoint® presentation. Students come to the Smart Board® to circle the title of the book and the spine label. Collaborate with teachers and use the Smart Board® within curriculum areas.

59. Microsoft Photo Story 3® Software

Grades: 3–8

ISTE (International Society for Technology in Education) National Education Technology Standards for Students
Content Standard III

Figure 6.11 National Standards for Microsoft Photo Story 3® Software

Microsoft Photo Story 3® software creates videos from pictures using simple, quick steps. Narration and music can also be easily inserted into the storyboard. Download Microsoft Photo Story 3® software for free from Microsoft®. Go to <www.microsoft.com>, click on "Downloads & Trials." After you have completed a story, save it as a Windows Media® Video (.wmv) and use a Windows Media Player® version 7 or later to view it.

Assessment Rubric

SKILL	LEVEL I Minimum	LEVEL II Average	LEVEL III Excellent
Does the student demonstrate understanding of the technology tool?			
Does the student use the technology tool to effectively communicate with peers?			

Figure 6.12 Photo Story 3® Software Assessment Rubric

Chapter 7

OUTRAGEOUS FUNDRAISERS

INTRODUCTION

Extra money for library books, projects, and special events can be garnered in unusual ways that are sure to attract attention. Sometimes the school district budget doesn't go as far as the "outrageous" librarian would like.

60. "Paws and Read" Book Club

Parents and students purchase books to honor pets. Place a photograph of the pet together with the book title on a bulletin board outside the library media center.

61. Book Race

Load a book truck with books and do laps. Ask local businesses and volunteer groups in the community to sponsor the race for a set amount of money per quarter mile.

62. Design a New "Library Doll"

Enough of the bun and glasses! Check out the January 2007 cover of *School Library Journal* for inspiration.

63. Library Store

Students design bookmarks, T-shirts, or posters focusing on reading. Items are then sold at lunch in the cafeteria.

64. Community Clean-Up Fundraiser

Choose a weekend day for the event. Students solicit pledges from family members and friends. Pledges are tied to number of pounds of trash collected. Individual students ask for a quarter for a pound of trash collected in the neighborhood. Set a maximum amount of $20 for each sponsor. Adults supervise groups of students for a two- hour collection. At the end weigh the results. With 100 students participating, collecting 10 pounds each with five sponsors, the final amount is $750.

Chapter 8

OUTRAGEOUS LIBRARY INSTRUCTION, BEHAVIOR MANAGEMENT, & PUBLICITY

INTRODUCTION

Library skills should always be incorporated into collaborative unit plans. However, at times specific skills and behaviors need to be addressed. Making the library skills memorable and instructive is the mantra of the "outrageous" librarian. Paths of knowledge and learning are more deeply embedded in memory while having fun!

65. Library Instruction with Gummy Worms®   Grades: K–8

Create a PowerPoint® presentation on the library use using Gummy Worms®, which can be purchased at local discount and grocery stores. Create slides that cover library behavior, shelf locations, and check-out and return procedures.

66. Dewey Alive   Grades: 2–5

Learn the Dewey Decimal System with dance, action steps, and poses. For example:

- 000 (world record books) – strike a weight lifting pose, followed by a verbal, "Ahhh," for wonderment.
- 100 – make sad, happy, excited, and frightened faces (dealing with emotions).
- 200 – place hands together, take two steps forward and bow your head.
- 300 – wear a wizard hat and say, "Once upon a time …"
- 400 – learn library in different languages.
- 500 – hold a plant and a toy animal.
- 600 – hold a light bulb and shout "Eureka! I invented it."
- 700 – be a football player with a paintbrush and sing.
- 800 – tell a poem or a joke.
- 900 – dress as a historical person.

67. Dewey Walk   Grades: 4–8

Everything has order. To demonstrate, take a walk outside or inside the school to classify objects the students see. Ideas include the kinds of trees, the colors or makes of cars, and the size of buildings around the school. Connect these with the different subject categories with the numerical system found in the Dewey Decimal Classification System. Place a card with the broad Dewey Decimal Classification number at the site of the object.

Library Orientation
with Gummy Worms®

Gummy Worms ▪ love to come to the
_____ Library.

BOOK CARE

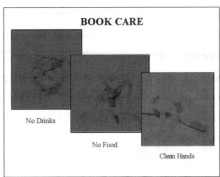

No Drinks

No Food

Clean Hands

LIBRARY BEHAVIOR

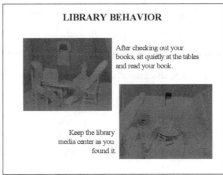

After checking out your
books, sit quietly at the tables
and read your book.

Keep the library
media center as you
found it.

LIBRARY ORGANIZATION

**Gummy Worms® learn that the library is
organized into three sections:**

Everybody   Fiction   Nonfiction

Everybody

Everybody books are
picture books with a
wide reading range.
Some are for students
just learning to read
and others are for more
advanced readers.

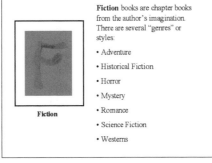

Fiction

Fiction books are chapter books
from the author's imagination.
There are several "genres" or
styles:

• Adventure
• Historical Fiction
• Horror
• Mystery
• Romance
• Science Fiction
• Westerns

Nonfiction

Nonfiction books contain facts
with the exception of some
books in the folktale and fairy
tale section (300), and the poetry
(800) section. They are arranged
according to the Dewey Decimal
Classification System. The
nonfiction section is organized
by numbers that tell the subject
of the book. For example, 741 is
found in the Art section. The
Dewey Decimal Systems
numbers range from 000 – 999.

ENJOY THE LIBRARY!

We are here to serve you!

Figure 8.1 Gummy Worm® Library Orientation

68. Dewey Flash

Ask fifth-grade teachers to collaborate on a photography project. Discuss the Dewey Decimal Classification System and its categories. Assign groups of four students to photograph items that belong in each major number group. For example, for the 700s, students can photograph paints, baseballs, footballs, soccer balls, and other items. Tell the students that only the best photographs will be accepted. Reward the winning group with extra library time, food coupons, or school supplies. Photographs will be printed and placed above the corresponding shelf.

69. Bowling for Dewey   Grades: 3–8

Buy plastic bowling pins and attach a Dewey number to each. After each person knocks down a pin or pins, have them choose one number to go locate the section. Students locate a title they like and report back to the whole classroom group.

BEHAVIOR MANAGEMENT

70. Boogie Line Up   Grades: PK–1

While students are lined up, sing the song to the tune "Hokey Pokey" and perform these words:

"Put your right foot out, put your left foot out, and do a shake, shake about."
"We do the Library Boogie in the school hall, glad you came to check us out!"
At the "shake, shake, about" students move with a wiggle out of the library.

71. Voice Modifier   All grades

Purchase a toy voice changer, such as one by Schylling®, available at <amazon.com>. Use different voices to grab attention. Watch students stop in mid-sentence and stare with a surprised look on their faces!

72. "R-E-A-D"   Grades: PK–2

Cue students with the letters to the word "READ."
   R = Ready?
   E = Ears listening
   A = Attention eyes
   D = Drop your hands in your lap

After training students a few weeks, watch as children quickly become quiet when the word "READ" is spoken.

73. Learn the Lingo

All grades

Try different languages to gain students' attention.

Silencio, por favor – Spanish (see-LIN-see-oh pour FAH-vor)

tranquillité, s'il vous plais – French (tran-keel-ee-TAY seel-VOO-play)

Ruhe, bitte – German (ROO-heh Bi-tuh)

Quiet, per favore – Italian (KEY-et per fah-VOR-eh)

Learn sign language for library directions:

For the word "quiet," the index finger is held up against pursed lips. Visit Simplified Signs Lexicon on the Web at <www.simplifiedsigns.org/lexicon.htm> for visual drawings of hand placement for other words in sign language.

LIBRARY PROMOTION

74. Bathroom Banter

Advertise the latest books in the library media center on the student and staff bathroom walls!

Materials

- Clear plastic sheet covers
- Paper

Directions

Type the title, "Flush Out These Titles From the Library," then list books that would appeal to boys and girls and place into a protective sheet cover. Tape the plastic sheet on the bathroom door or walls.

75. Cafeteria Library Lady

Plagued by cafeteria duty? Turn a negative into a positive by advertising books. Buy an apron and sew plastic vinyl pockets large enough to hold books. Wear a tall hat with a sign that says, "Have You Read These?" Grab a microphone and read one aloud.

Figure 8.2 Cafeteria Librarian

Chapter 9

FINAL THOUGHTS

"What do you do to promote literacy in your library?" author Pat Mora asked me as I stood in front of her at the author's autograph table at a recent Texas Library Association Convention. Shocked that I

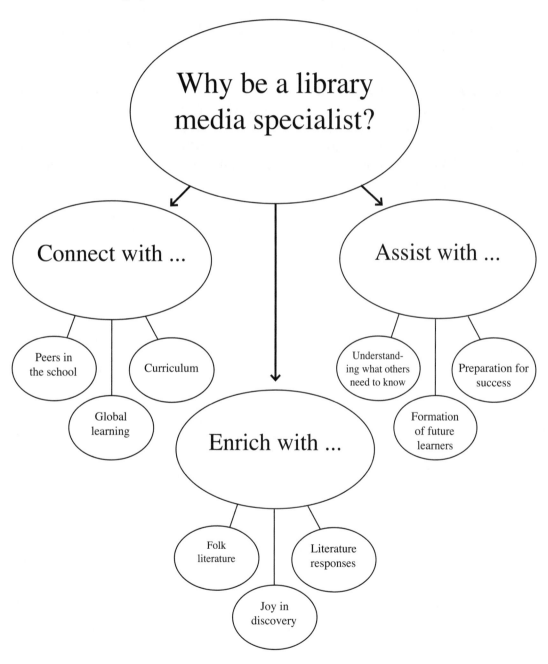

Figure 9.1 Why Be a Library Media Specialist?

was being asked a question by this wonderful author, I stammered out a few words about reading contests. I realized I did not have the words to describe all the things I do to excite students about literacy in the library media center. That question sent me back to consider the basics of my purpose as a library media specialist. I created a Web to consider my role.

As I sketched out my basic thoughts and desires in my profession, it dawned on me that my greatest joy was the understanding of what others need to know and seeing the joy in the discovery of new knowledge. This pause, or break, that Pat Mora's question offered centered my future professional outlook. Our special position in the school provides the opportunity to reflect upon what are the key, essential components of knowledge of various subject matters and the ability to concretely convey this to our fellow teachers and students in collaborative events. I realized that promoting literacy *and student achievement* quite naturally go hand in hand. When we library media specialists link text, technology, and activity to curriculum standards, we are spreading our literacy cloak that we all wear as librarians, to encompass the whole school.

The time of reflection also sent me on a quest to go where no library media specialist has ever gone to promote student learning and achievement. No action or activity on my part could be too embarrassing! It is work, as I find time to understand and incorporate essential knowledge and outcomes in my collaborations. However, it is never boring, as I take each component and attempt to make it fun and of course, outrageous fun! What I discovered was complete joy and a new lease on my life as a school library media specialist. I highly recommend becoming an "outrageous" librarian!

WORKS CITED

Werner, Linnette and Freeman, Carol J. "Arts for Academic Achievement: Arts Integration–A Vehicle for Changing Teacher Practice." Presented at the annual meeting of the American Educational Research Association, Seattle, OR. April 2001.

SUGGESTED PROFESSIONAL RESOURCES

Aims Education Foundation. *Science Core Curriculum*. Fresno: Aims Education Foundation, 2007.

De Las Casas, Dianne. *Kamishibai Story Theater: The Art of Picture Telling*. Westport: Teacher Ideas Press, 2006.

Grimes, Sharon. *Reading is Our Business: How Libraries Can Foster Reading Comprehension*. Chicago: American Library Association, 2006.

Harvey, Stephanie. *Nonfiction Matters: Reading, Writing, and Research in Grades 3 – 8*. Portland: Stenhouse Publishers, 1998.
Strategies That Work: Teaching Comprehension for Understanding and Encouragement, 2nd edition. Portland: Stenhouse Publishers, 2007.

Koch, Kenneth and Ron Padgett. *Wishes, Lies, and Dreams: Teaching Children to Write Poetry*. New York: Harper Paperbacks, 2000.

Morris, Alana. *Vocabulary Unplugged: 30 Lessons That Will Revolutionize How You Teach Vocabulary K – 12*. Shoreham: Discover Writing Press, 2005.

Vardell, Sylvia M. *Poetry Aloud Here! Sharing Poetry with Children in the Library*. Chicago: American Library Association, 2006.

Wormeli, Rick. *Summarization in Any Subject: 50 Techniques to Improve Student Learning*. Alexandria: Association for Supervision & Curriculum Development, 2005.

Worthy, Jo. Readers *Theater for Building Fluency: Strategies and Scripts for Making the Most of This Highly Effective, Motivating and Research-Based Approach to Oral Reading*. Teaching Strategies, 2005.

Zaslavsky, Claudia. *Math Games & Activities from Around the World*. Chicago: Chicago Review Press, 1998.

INDEX